Schindler's

Tiny Tales

And

Whatnot

By

James A. Schindler

ISBN: 1-4140-0485-0 (e-book)
ISBN: 1-4140-0484-2 (Paperback)
ISBN: 1-4140-0483-4 (Dust Jacket)

Library of Congress Control Number: 2003096706

This book is printed on acid free paper.

Printed in the United States of America
Bloomington, IN

1stBooks – rev. 04/26/04

A Point of Interest

All the tiny tales in this book are based on true stories as I remember them, or as were told to me by the people involved. Some are slightly embellished, but none are made up.

I would like to thank my wife, children, relatives, friends, and the others who were either in the stories or told me their tales.

As far as I know, the comments or "Whatnots" are my own. However, somewhere in the back of my mind is stored so much information that I have read, heard, or run across in my sixty-plus years, that if I have inadvertently said or written something that has already been said or written, I apologize, since I have neither the time nor inclination to research each and every comment or saying.

Some of the "Tiny Tales" and "Whatnots" may be a little risqué and controversial. However, if anyone is so prudish as to take offense, I would like to point out that although these pages are not absorbent enough for any other purpose, they are highly combustible!

Schindler's
Tiny Tales and Whatnot

Spankin' Shirley

In the early nineteen sixties, my oldest brother, Chico, and I were sitting in Blackstone's Bar, having a couple of beers, when he said, "I got madder than hell at Shirley [his wife] last night."

"You did?" I asked.

"Yeah," he replied. "I was so damn mad that I put her across my knee to give her a spankin'…but by the time I got her pants down, I wasn't mad anymore!"

Running Nose

In my youth, I probably spent more time at Blackstone's Bar than I should have. Again, I was sitting with Chico (his given name was Eugene) and I said, "I can't shake this damn cold. I've had it for a month and my nose won't quit running!"

Chico glanced at me and then nonchalantly said, "It's big enough, it ought'a have legs!"

The Purple Hooter

Tonight we had our monthly manager meeting at the Outback restaurant and, after dinner, Anil Doshi, Bandido's VP, ordered cheesecake with a raspberry glacé. The waitress told us that the raspberry glacé was imported from France and was made with

Chambord, an expensive raspberry liqueur. Then she brought us a shot of Chambord so we could taste it. Jim Horton, our Lima manager, said, "Oh yeah, we use this to make Purple Hooters."

"Purple Hooters?" I questioned.

"Yeah," he replied, "Don't you know how to make a Purple Hooter?"

"Sure," I said, "You just squeeze'em real hard!"

Just Maybe

A few years ago, I had just come home from work, and my kids, Rachel (5), Heidi (7), and Jimmie (8), ran up to meet me for their customary hugs and kisses. The children then followed me into the house and into the bathroom. I noticed that one side of the curtain, rod and all, had been pulled out of the wall. The window was small and high, and on the floor beneath it was a hot water baseboard heater. It was apparent that one of the kids had stood on the heater and grabbed the curtain to pull him or herself up so he or she could see out of the window, and had torn the rod out of the wall.

Now I must explain that, being the monster that I am, I told the kids as they were growing up that if I ever caught them lying or stealing, they would, without a doubt, get a spankin', and that I would never spank them if they told the truth. So I turned and looked at all three of them standing there and said, "Who pulled the curtain down? Jimmie, did you do it?"

He shook his head and said, "I didn't do it."

"Heidi, did you do it?"

Same reaction, and also, "I didn't do it."

Rachel stood there, with this guilty-as-sin look on her face, as I turned to her and asked, "Did you do it?" She looked me right in the eye and said, as she put her hands on her hips and her weight on one foot, "Maybe I did [she then shifted her weight to the other foot], and maybe I didn't!"

Lying Eyes

Sometimes, when I go into one of my Bandido's Mexican Restaurants and see something that isn't the way that it's supposed to be and the manager or employee says, "I don't know what happened; it's never like that," I tell them this story.

There was once a man making love to his girlfriend when his wife walked in. As soon as he saw her, he jumped out of bed, ran up to her and said. "Honey, are you going to believe me or your lying eyes?"

Words of Wisdom

When my son John was growing up, he was real quiet. One day, he must have been around nine years old; we were driving over to my brother's house. After about ten minutes of silence I asked, "John, why don't you ever say anything?"

He looked at me, paused, and then said, "I will when I have something to say!"

Nuuuuns!!!...Nuuuuns!!!

John was five in the summer of 1970, and one of his favorite TV programs was "The Flying Nun." One sunny day, as he was sitting on the porch at our house on Second St. in Decatur, two nuns from St. Joseph's Catholic School (they still dressed in the full length black habits back then) came walking by. As soon as he spotted them, he jumped off the porch and ran after them shouting, "Nuuuns...nuuuns!" They turned around, saw this little boy coming lickety-split towards them and waited for him to catch up. As soon as he did, he looked up at them and shouted excitedly, "Can you fly?"

In the Be-grinning!

One evening, about five years ago, my wife Fry and I took Father Tony, a priest friend of ours, to Henry's Bar for dinner. Father Tony is from Sri Lanka, and although he understands English very well, he is not familiar with many of the local phrases and idioms.

After we'd finished eating, we were relaxing and having an after-dinner drink when Fry excused herself to go to the ladies room. As soon as she disappeared from sight, I leaned across the table towards Father Tony and said in a semi-whisper, "Father, I'm worried about Fry."

"Why, what's the matter?" he asked with a puzzled look.

"She is really getting religious," I said in a hushed tone.

"She is?"

"Yes, last night when we were in bed, she kept yelling, 'Ohhhhhh God! Ohhhhhh Jesus!'"

Now it was obvious, by the perplexed expression on his face, that Father Tony didn't get it. But in a moment it began to sink in, and soon a very slight grin began to appear on his face. With each second it slowly got bigger and bigger until he was grinning from ear to ear!

Barge Pole Joe

In the 1950s, Joe was in the U.S. Air Force, stationed in England. Like many young airmen, he liked to drink, rev up his engine and have a good time. One night out on the town, he found himself with a couple of his buddies in a house of easy virtue. After a short but successful negotiation with one of the ladies, they went to a room and promptly disrobed. While he was standing there in great anticipation, she took one look at him and blurted out, "My God, man, where did you get that barge pole?"

At that moment Joe puffed up like a horny toad, and his buddies still swear to this day, that when he came out of that room, he stood at least two inches taller! You might say that he grew on her!

Never—Never

Never let anyone put their hand into your pocket or purse,

Unless you know how much they're going to take!

Partnership

When I was in the seventh grade, an old farmer who lived next door gave me this advice. I can still recall it, even though at that time I didn't understand what he meant and I wondered why he was telling it to me. He said, "Son, always remember, <u>Partnership is a poor ship to sail!</u>" How I wish I had listened to that old man, because it could have saved me a lot of rough sailing!

The Long and Short of it!

A short time ago, I was standing in our kitchen next to my sixteen-year-old son, Jimmie, who is over 6'1'' (I'm only 5'11''). You know how you can sense when someone is looking at you? Well, I looked up at him, and he had this big grin on his face as he looked down at me and proudly exclaimed, "Dad, I'm taller than you!"

"You're right, son," I said, "But I'm longer!"

After a brief pause, he looked at me and replied, "In your dreams!"

Oh, Were It True!

My wife Fry and I were having a discussion about something which I can't recall at the moment, and after I had described what happened, she said, "That's not what happened," and went on to give her version of the story. When she finished, she said, "Now that's the way it was! Remember...I have the memory of an elephant!"

"Yeah," I smirked, "but I have the trunk of one!"

After her laughter died down, I continued, "But I can't pick up a peanut with it!"

Here's Lookin' at You!

One day a lady friend of mine went to her gynecologist for a routine checkup. While he was examining her, he said, "What do you do for a living?"

"Oh," she said, "I'm an oral hygienist."

"My God," he exclaimed "How can you stand looking into people's mouths all day?"

"Well, what do you look at all day?"

"Now that's a dirty crack," he replied.

"Hey, let's not get personal!" she said indignantly.

Fruit for Thought

A peach is just a peach,

But it's hard to beat a nice pair!

Freddy's Optimism

I had breakfast this morning with an old high school buddy, Freddy Eyanson. He told me that he had leukemia, but said it wasn't the bad kind.

"Why," he exclaimed, "I'll probably outlive it!"

The Gift of a Loan

Whenever I lend money to my family or friends, in my mind's eye, I see it as a gift. Then if I get paid back, I'm pleasantly surprised. But if I don't, since I saw it as a gift, I never become embittered or angry, for to lose their friendship over a few dollars seems foolish to me!

Mistakes

There are two kinds of people who never make mistakes. The first kind never does anything, and the second kind is dead! Anyone who does anything at all will make them. So I never worry about making a mistake, but as soon as I realize that I did, I just try to correct it as quickly as possible.

Back from the Front

Did you ever notice that when you go into the front of a church,

you're in the back? And the more up front you go,

the farther back you are!

The Good Framer

Recently, I bought a painting, and as I was paying for it, the clerk asked if I would like it framed.

"Who's going to frame it?" I asked.

"I am," she replied.

"Are you any good?"

"I'm fabulous," she answered. "There is only one person better than me, and he taught me how, but he's retired now."

"Well," I quipped. "If you're that good, you must be frameous!"

A Clean Ending

If all the paperwork in the world was put on highly
absorbent sheets, two ends could be served!

No Principals

One day, shortly after my sister-in-law, Mary Keefer, was
appointed principal of Bishop Luers High School, I called her to
congratulate her on her new position.

"Mary," I said, "Congratulations! I didn't know you had any,
and now you are one!"

The Big V

My daughter Rachel was born when I was fifty years old. She
was a beautiful and healthy child, just like our first two, and I have no
regrets. However, because of my age, I decided that she would be the
last of my loins, and I'd have a vasectomy.

The scheduled time came, and I was lying on the table in Dr.
Schlueter's office, listening to him describe the procedure to me.
When he finished, he asked if I had any questions.

"Doc," I said, "I just want you to remember one thing."

"What's that?"

"I'm the vasectomy; the next guy's the castration!"

He smiled and started the procedure. He gave me a local so I
couldn't feel anything but just a slight pulling in my groin area. Then,
all of a sudden, I heard him say, "Ooops!"

"What happened?" I asked with a little panic in my voice.

"We're even," he laughed.

Average

There's only one thing wrong with being average. It's so common!

The Face on the Bar Room Bore

In 1966, I was 32 years old, and for the first time in my life I grew a beard. I kept it well trimmed and, frankly, I thought that I looked quite handsome in it. One day, as my wife and I were having dinner and a few drinks at Tony's Tap, a local watering hole in Decatur, some friends of ours, Tom and Peg Sefton, joined us. After the usual exchange of pleasantries, Peg looked at me and said, "I really like your beard."

"You do?" I replied, hoping to hear more.

"Yes," she continued, "It hides so much of your face!"

Twice

"I made a mistake once."

"You did?"

"Yeah, I got married twice!"

Uppis

Definition: What a person is suffering from
when he goes around with his head uppis derriere.

The Boot

When my son John was about eight years old, every Saturday he would help me work in the yard. He'd pick up sticks and do other odd jobs while I mowed the grass. One day, the mower ran out of fuel and I sent John to get the gas can. After about ten minutes, he still hadn't returned, and I wondered what was taking him so long. I walked over to the garage and there he stood, his back to me and his mind dreaming of everything except the job at hand. I then booted him in the butt with the instep of my shoe. Not hard enough to hurt him, but hard enough to get his attention. The blow startled him back to reality and he grabbed the gas can. This happened on at least two or three different Saturdays.

A short time after that, we went to a wedding. One of my friends saw John and just by chance remarked, "Hi, John, anyone boot you in the butt today?"

"No," John answered. He then took a few steps, stopped, turned around and said, "And that's unusual for a Saturday!"

Let's Go Bowling

About three and a half weeks ago, I had prostate surgery. A few days later, I missed my check-up because of other commitments. Today, I called my urologist with some questions that I had. The receptionist said, "I'm sorry; Dr. Schlueter is not in, but I'll connect you with Karen, his nurse."

A short pause, then, "Hello."

"Is this Karen?"

"Yes, it is."

"Karen, this is Mr. Schindler, and I have a couple of questions."

"Okaaay," she said, trying to draw them out.

"First, can I go bowling? And secondly, I mean, it's been a long dry spell, can I have sex?"

"Dr. Schlueter is out of town, but he will call in later this morning, and I'll ask him. Give me your phone number, and I'll call you back."

I gave her my number, said goodbye and went to the office. About an hour or so later my wife Fry called me and said, "I just heard from Schlueter's office."

"Well, what did they say?" I wanted to know.

"They had good news and bad news," she teased.

"Tell me the good news," I said with great anticipation.

"The good news is…you can go bowling!"

Nobody's Perfect

Two weeks and two days after the good news-bowling incident, I had another appointment with Dr. Schlueter. I went through the usual routine, giving my best sample in a tiny paper cup, and was then sent into a small examining room. In a few minutes, the doctor came in.

"How are you doing?" he asked.

"I'm doing great. No pain; everything is working fine."

"I could tell by your urine sample," he said. "You don't need to see me for another year. I'll have the nurse make an appointment. Do you have any questions?"

"Can I have sex now?"

"Sure," he grinned.

"Doc, being a good Catholic, I have a confession to make."

"You do?"

"Yeah... I cheated."

That's Fast

"How fast are you?"

"I'm so fast...that it makes my wife mad!"

The Mirror on Caesar's Ceiling

In the early 1980s, my wife and I went to Las Vegas and stayed at Caesar's Palace. As we entered our room, the first thing that we noticed was a round bed with a round mirror on the ceiling directly above it. While we were commenting on the mirror and bed, we heard a knock on the door.

"Who is it?" I yelled.

"The maid," was the reply.

"Go away," I said, "We're looking in the mirror!"

We both broke out laughing. I then walked over and opened the door. The maid was gone!

Later, as we lay in bed, I wondered if someone could be above the mirror with a camera, which inspired me to write the following poem:

Mirror, Mirror, on Caesar's Ceiling

Mirror, mirror, on Caesar's ceiling,

Is there something you're concealing?

As I lie here with my love true,

Could there be someone above you?

With their camera pointed down,

Getting shots from toe to crown.

Every detail of our moving,

Caught on film for later viewing.

Then one day in my hometown,

It was seen and passed around.

With us bare for all to view,

If we knew we were Stars,

We'd have waved at you!!!

Not So Fast, Doc

Last week, my thirteen-year-old daughter Rachel went in for back surgery. A few minutes before she was to be wheeled into the operating room, Dr. Buchholtz came in to explain the procedure to us. He told us what he was going to do, and then said that the surgery

15

usually took about three hours. He also explained that since Dr. LaSalle was going to assist him, he felt that he would be finished in about an hour and a half. Rachel was listening intently, but when he said that, she raised her head off the cart, looked at the good doctor and said, "Don't rush it!"

No Mas

Remember when fast food was?

No Crap

In any business, quality is paramount.
The only way that you can be successful selling crap
is if you're in the fertilizer business!

We're Not There Yet!

The whole transportation industry is based on the
simple premise that everybody wants to be where they ain't!

No Direction

In the summer of 1946, my brother Joe was 14, I was 12, and we were living with a farmer, LB Myers, outside of Elyria, Ohio. One Sunday, he wanted to visit another farmer he had heard of, to inquire about a particular brand of seed corn. So with address in hand, and Joe and I in tow, he set off.

Up and down, and back and forth on those potholed, graveled country roads he drove, looking for that farm. Finally, after an hour or so, in sheer frustration, LB spotted an old man working in his barnyard and stopped for directions. It was obvious by his weathered face, gnarled hands and bib overalls, that he was hard working and down to earth. (In those days, farmers wore bib overalls, and kids wouldn't have been caught dead in them!)

"Say," LB said, "could you tell me how to find Billy Booster's place on Dutchman's Road?"

"On Dutchman's Road?" he repeated.

Yep," LB answered.

"Billy Booster's place, huh?"

Another, "Yep."

The old guy looked at the ground, rubbed the stubble on his chin with his thumb and forefinger, and repeated, as much for his own ears as ours, "Bill Booster's place, Dutchman's Road…huh?"

Requiring still another "Yep," from LB.

After a brief pause, he squinted at us in a state of confused bewilderment and blurted out, "Why…why…you can't get there from here!"

Too Small for my Britches

About two years after our marriage, my wife was bending over, cleaning off the table, when I walked into the kitchen.

"My," I said, noticing her derrière, "we've picked up a few pounds, haven't we?"

"What do you mean? I weigh the same as I did when we got married!" she replied.

"Aw, come on, I'll bet your rear's bigger than mine."

"No, it's not!" she exclaimed emphatically, as she gave me a wounded look. Realizing that I had just stuck my foot in my mouth, I retreated to the living room to catch up on my TV time.

Being an insensitive slob, I soon forgot all about our little conversation, when in she marched, and stood between the TV and me, wearing a pair of my pants. Pulling them out at the waist to show me that they were obviously too big, she announced excitedly, "See...see, I told you so. Your pants are too big for me!"

It took me a brief moment to get over this surprise development, but when I did, I pointed my index finger at her and said, "And don't you ever forget it!"

I'm Here

Sometimes when I'm at a restaurant, the server will deliver the food, set it down, and say, "There you go."

I then reply, "Where do I go? I thought I was here!"

The Book That Made An Impression

In the nineteen sixties, my stepdaughter Laurie was in the second grade at Adams Central School. One day she brought home a note from her teacher, Mrs. Davis. It said that during class Laurie would talk, get up and look out the window, and was disruptive in general. Mrs. Davis went on to say that she was at her wits' end and didn't know what to do.

That evening, I sat down and wrote Mrs. Davis the following note.

Dear Mrs. Davis,

Regarding Laurie:

Why don't you take your psychology book and apply it with some force to the seat of the problem?

Sincerely yours,

Jim Schindler

P.S. This must have made a lasting impression on Laurie, for Mrs. Davis never felt the need to write me again!

What Does He Know?

In 1968, a friend Tom Hurst and I were working on an electro-mechanical device. We contacted a hotshot engineer from the Magnavox Company, who came highly recommended, to put it together for us. We described it to him and explained what it was supposed to do. He then told us that he'd get back to us as soon as he had a chance to think it over.

About a week later, Tom and I met with him to see what he had decided. He said, "I hate to disappoint you guys, but there is no way that this damn thing will work. I'm telling you as an engineer, you can't make something like that. There's no way. It won't work!"

"Are you sure?" Tom asked.

"I'm positive."

"Well," I said, "if you can't do it, do you know somebody who could?"

Sensing that we were not about to give up, he said, "There's a guy in Hoagland who has a little machine shop, and he doesn't know that it can't be done. Maybe he can do it for you."

Moral: If you don't know you can't...you can!

Honey, Wag the Tail

One day in 1975, I had just come home from work. Domino, the family dog, ran up to me. I scratched him behind the ears and headed towards the house. As I was reaching for the knob, the door swung open and there stood my wife, and boy, was she upset about something. She was standing on the inside of the threshold and I was on the outside, as she began to give me an old fashioned tongue-lashing.

As I stood there, I could feel Domino nudge me with his nose and I reached down and again scratched him behind the ear, as his tail swung happily back and forth. Meanwhile, my wife kept on giving me what-for, as I listened silently, petting Domino. Finally, she stopped, apparently finished with her tirade. (Experience has taught me that if you don't fuel the fire by commenting or arguing, the kettle will soon run out of steam!)

I glanced at her, then at the dog, and said, "Why can't you be more like Domino?"

"What do you mean?" she asked warily.

"If you'd wag your tail instead of your damn tongue when I get home, we'd get along a lot better!"

The door slammed. I felt like an outsider…and the only tail that wagged for many a day at our household was that of my old friend Domino.

A Real Dog's Life

Domino, our family pet, was the best dog that I ever had. He was a mixed breed, mostly hound, and was very friendly and intelligent. He had the run of our small city and the surrounding countryside. Neighbors would tell me that they spotted him as far as fifteen or twenty miles away. You might say that he had a roving eye and just loved those bitches.

Sometimes, he would take off and be gone for up to two weeks. When he came home he would lie around for days, recuperating and regaining his virility. His healing time seemed to be in direct proportion to the number of days that he had spent on his amorous pursuits. Once rested, he would spend a few days around the house before he'd begin his next quest.

On a warm spring day, the doorbell rang. I opened it, and beheld a very irritated man who lived about three blocks away. He explained that he had a bitch in heat, caged in his back yard to protect her noble bloodline while she was in that condition. He went on to say that last night Domino had torn the cage apart and proceeded to charm her. He then informed me in very graphic terms what he would do if he ever caught him on his property again.

"Don't worry," I assured him, "I'll give him exactly what he deserves."

With that promise, he seemed satisfied and left. I walked back into the house, closed the door, and called Domino over to me. I petted him, scratched him behind the ears, and said, "Congratulations, Domino, I think you're going to be a father."

Domino never knew a leash or chain. He spent his entire fifteen years roaming the countryside looking for love and living a dog's life. In 1986, he died in his sleep. What a dog!

No Golf Today

My good friend Heinrich Husmann came over from Germany in 1954. He followed his sweetheart, Anne, who had moved here a year or two sooner. When he arrived in the U.S., he had twenty-one dollars and sixty cents in his pocket and could not speak a word of English. Heinrich was a hard worker and soon found a job laying out and painting billboards for a dollar and a quarter an hour. In a year or so, he was hired to paint houses at four dollars and seventy-five cents an hour. When the boss found out that he could paint murals, and saw the good work that he did, his wages jumped to six dollars and twenty-five cents. Not bad in those days.

Heinrich learned English by reading the newspaper and watching TV. It wasn't long before he and Anne were married and started a family. After a few years of hard work, he decided to open his own decorating business. Because of his talent, dedication, long hours and sheer determination, he became quite successful. He had a nice family, a fine house, a neat boat, an airplane and all the trappings of a successful businessman.

One day, while visiting a couple of his friends, he was asked, "Henry [his American friends found it a lot easier just to call him Henry], how in the hell did you do it? You came over here with virtually no money; you couldn't even speak English, and now look at you. You've done better than most of the people who have lived here all their lives. How'd you do it?"

Henry then told them this story. "Every morning when I leave the house, I stop for coffee with the boys for a hour or so, then I go and play a round of golf. After lunch, we play another round of golf and then stop at the club house for a drink or two."

"Wait a minute," one of his friends exclaimed, "I never saw you on the golf course!"

"Now you've got it!" Henry said emphatically.

A Handy Lesson

In the late nineteen thirties, when Heinrich was a young lad, he was working with his father. He was no different than most teenage boys and thought he knew just about everything worth knowing. One day, his father had had enough of his know-it-all attitude. But experience and the passing years had given him much wisdom, so instead of getting angry with Heinrich, he said, "Son, come here. Hold up your hand."

Heinrich did as he was asked.

"Now look at your hand."

23

Again Heinrich did as his father requested.

"When all five fingers are the same length," he said, "then you will know everything!"

Heinrich never forgot this handy lesson.

You SOB

Bill was in bad shape. Not only did he have heart problems, but he was also suffering from diabetes. His circulation in one leg was so bad that they had to amputate it. Diane, his wife, adored him and worked two jobs to support him and the two kids.

It should have been no surprise when she got a call at work from her daughter, but it was. "Mom," she cried, "They've taken Dad to St. Joseph's Hospital; he's having chest pains."

"I'll run right over," she said in a panic.

When she arrived at the hospital, she ran up to the intensive care room where Bill was lying conscious. He was attached to several IVs, supplied from plastic bags hanging from a rack, and there were tubes stuck into almost every orifice of his body. Several monitors were checking his vital signs.

Diane was so distraught that she rushed up to him with tears in her eyes, put her arms around him and said, "Bill, you son of a bitch, if you die on me, I'm gonna kill ya!"

Epilogue: Bill's doing just fine now. I guess he just didn't want to get killed!

They are Us!

Many years ago, Pogo, a comic strip by Walt Kelly, which ran in our local paper, pointed out the obvious to me. It went something like this. The first frame showed Albert the alligator running out of the swamp, yelling, "Help…help!"

The second picture showed him standing next to his friend Pogo, who said, "What's the matter, Albert?"

He replied, "I have met the enemy."

In the third and final picture, Pogo said, "You did?"

"Yes," Albert continued, "and they are us!"

Jimmie's Up!

There is a short hallway that leads from our kitchen to a bathroom. On the right, just before you get to the bathroom, is my sixteen-year-old son Jimmie's bedroom. My thirteen-year-old daughter Rachel and I were having breakfast together one morning when, unbeknownst to us, Jimmie got up and went into the bathroom and didn't shut the door all the way. (You can't see the bathroom from the kitchen table). Now young boys are known for their pressure, and when he started to splash and churn the water in the stool, we could hear it all the way in the kitchen. Rachel, nonchalantly, between bites, glanced at me and said, "Boy, you can sure tell when Jimmie's up!"

No Matter How You Doctor It

You can't have a "First Class Operation"
with second-class people!

Reflection

Matt had been working for me at Bandido's Mexican Restaurant for roughly ten years. All through that time he had troubles with drinking, gambling, women, cars and you name it. He always had a hundred excuses as to why bad things happened to him, and blamed everyone but himself.

One morning, as I walked into the restaurant, he started out with his "poor me, nobody ever helps me" bit, and began placing the blame everywhere but where it belonged. I said, "Matt [who just happens to be black], do you really want to know who is the cause of all your troubles?"

He looked at me quizzically, and replied, "Yeah."

"Come into the bathroom with me, and I'll show you."

Matt followed me into the men's room. "Stand right here," I told him, as I positioned him in front of the mirror, so that the only person he could see was himself.

"Do you see that guy in the mirror?" I asked, "He's the cause of all your troubles."

Matt looked intently into the mirror, moving his head from one side to the other, trying to find the one responsible. "I don't see anybody," he said.

"Look again, Matt. Don't you see that black guy right in front of you?"

"Oh, you mean me?" he said, somewhat surprised.

"Yes," I said. "He's the SOB that got you drunk, wrecked your car and got you arrested for DUI. He's the guy that lost all your money, gambling. Matt, you can go on blaming everyone else, but until you admit that the guy in the mirror is the cause of your troubles, things aren't going to get any better for you. Nobody's to blame but him," I shouted, as I pointed at his reflection in the mirror.

"Oh, I see what you mean," he said in amazement. I don't think that it had ever occurred to him before that he was the problem, and as I watched his expression, I hoped that it was finally sinking in.

"You see, Matt, when you blame your problems on someone or something else, there is nothing that you can do about them, because it's not your fault. You can't change your friends, your boss, the weather, God, or whatever your excuse is, if it's not your fault. But when you admit that you're to blame, then, and only then, can you do something about it. Anytime that you really want to know who your best friend or worst enemy is, just look into the mirror. The reflection that you see, depending on your actions and decisions, is either your best friend or worst enemy. It's up to you!"

Car 29, Help Is On The Way!

My mind was a million miles away as I sped down a suburban street. The beeping of my fuzz buster brought me back to reality, but not before the police officer had already timed me. He was sitting on a side street with his radar gun aimed at me as I drove by. I glanced in my rear mirror, hoping that he hadn't caught me, but I knew better. He whipped onto the road, lights flashing and siren squealing like the pig I now thought he was.

I pulled over, stopped and waited for him. He walked up to my car and said, "May I see you driver's license and registration?" I fished them out of the glove box and handed them over. "I clocked you doing fifty, and the speed limit is only thirty-five."

He then went back to his car. I knew he had seen my fuzz buster, and I was sure that he was going to give me a ticket.

In a few minutes, he again approached my car. "Here is your registration and license. Would you sign this ticket, please?"

I did as he requested and handed it back to him. He gave me a copy, and explained my options. Then he looked directly at me and said, "Mr. Schindler, why the fuzz buster?"

"Do you want to know why I have it?" I asked.

"Yes, sir," he answered.

"I have it so I know where the police are. Then, if they get into trouble, I can help them out!"

The Good Spirits

My daughter Rachel is in the eighth grade at St. John the Baptist Catholic School in Fort Wayne, and yesterday was her Confirmation. (The sacrament of Confirmation is when one receives the gift of the Holy Spirit). Bishop Jenky of South Bend was scheduled to perform the ceremony. At four o'clock the church was packed, and everyone was waiting for mass to begin.

Five minutes after four, I glanced at my watch. At ten after, Father Kummer, the parish priest, walked over to the pulpit and told the congregation that the Bishop was not there yet, but they expected him at any moment. At twenty after, the ceremony began. The procession, led by the Bishop in his official garb, marched down the aisle and all took their places in the sanctuary. It was an impressive sight, with the Bishop wearing the traditional vestments with miter (pointed hat), and carrying a shepherd's staff.

He began by saying, "I apologize; I thought that I knew Fort Wayne, but we got lost. We were talking, and I must have taken a wrong turn. We drove around some, looking for you, and then we stopped at a gas station to ask directions, but they didn't know where St. John's was. We pulled in two more gas stations, and they'd never heard of you! So we drove some more and came upon a liquor store. In desperation, we decided to ask them. They knew exactly where St. John's was!"

P.S. Does this mean that Saint John's congregation had already received its spirits?

Have You Seen the Plum Jam?

In the nineteen fifties, one of my brother Joe's best friends in the Air Force was a guy named Willis. Every so often his mother would send him a shipment of her homemade plum jam. He would always share it with his close buddies and everyone really liked it.

One night, Joe and the guys were lying in their bunks, shooting the bull. While they were waiting for the sandman, they started to tease and ridicule Willis about something. They kept it up even more, when it became obvious that they were getting his goat. Finally, he'd had enough. He was so upset that he wanted to get back at them. So he said, "If you guys don't knock it off, I'm not going to give you any more of my mom's plum jam!"

"You know what you can do with your plum jam?" Joe asked.

"What?" Willis answered.

"You can take your plum jam, and jam it plum up your ass."

Sit

Did you ever notice that when you were a kid,

everyone told you to sit up, and now that

you've grown up, they tell you to sit down?

Do you really give a sit?

What's Tat?

Some people believe in "tit for tat."

Quite frankly, I prefer it the other way around!

Busy, Huh?

Whenever I go into one of my restaurants, and the manager is

standing there with his hands in his pockets, I say to him,

"I'd shake your hand, but I see you're busy!"

or

"I'm always suspicious of a guy with both hands

in his pockets, and a big grin on his face."

or

"It's nice to see that you've got ahold of yourself."

then

You should see how fast they yank their hands out.

They usually smile at me, but they get the point.

I very rarely have to use that line on them again.

I found that using humor to teach a lesson

has a more pleasant and lasting effect than most other methods.

Here's To Ya!

Bill "Mad Dog" Mooney managed one of my pizza restaurants a few years ago. His grandmother lived in Germany, and she was getting along in years and wanted to see him. Being fairly well off financially, she sent him some money to buy a round trip-ticket to visit her. Of course, being young, footloose and fancy-free, Mad Dog looked at this windfall and had a serious decision to make. He could go see Grandma or succumb to the overwhelming desire to party with his friends. Thus he reasoned with himself. "If I go to Germany, the Skinheads don't like foreigners and I could get into serious trouble. It's also possible that I could have a bad flight, get airsick, and who knows what might happen to the plane. Now I don't think that Grandma wants me to put myself in that kind of a dangerous situation, so I better talk this over with my friends."

Needless to say, Mad Dog met his buddies, and together they took the Saturday night flight to the Boom Boom Saloon, their local hang out. (Temptation is always irresistible when it's self-induced).

A few weeks later Grandma phoned, "Bill," she said, "I haven't heard from you. Are you coming over to see me?"

"I can't, Grandma," he said sheepishly.

"Why not?" she wanted to know.

"I spent the money you sent."

Now Grandma wasn't wealthy because she was a fool, so she said, "Bill, I want to see you; this might be my last chance. I'll send you a round-trip ticket, and when you get here I'll give you some spending money." She sent the ticket, and Mad Dog made the trip.

Two weeks later, on a Monday morning, he walked into my office. "Mad Dog," I shouted, "When did you get back?"

"Late last night."

"Did you have a good time?"

"Great," he replied. "I brought you something from Germany."

"You did?" I said quizzically, since he had come into my office empty-handed.

"Yeah, it's a real good bottle of German booze."

"Where is it?" I asked.

"I drank it on the plane," he said with an impish grin.

Happiness

I honestly believe that most folks think that their happiness is dependent on someone or something that they have no control over. We've all heard people say, "I'd be happy if only…I won the lottery, or if I could find a good woman (or man), or if I had a better job, or a college education, or lived in Hawaii or California, then I'd be happy."

No, they won't! Things or places can't make them happy. If that were the case, then all millionaires would be happy. After all, can't they afford the things they want? If places make people happy, then everyone who lives in California, Hawaii, or one of the garden spots of the world, would always be smiling and content. But we all know that this isn't true.

Almost fifteen years ago, I was at my thirty-fifth class reunion, when I asked one of my classmates if they ever heard from Johnny, one of our old school chums.

"Don't you know what happened to Johnny?" he remarked.

"No," I replied, "What happened?"

"About three years ago, Johnny killed himself out in California."

"He did?"

"Yep, put a bullet in his head."

I don't really know why Johnny did it, but here's what I think transpired. In the 1950s, we attended Decatur Catholic High School together, and Johnny was a couple of grades behind me. How we got along, I'll never know, because he was always complaining. He told me that he hated Decatur, the people in it, and he couldn't wait until he graduated so he could move to California, where the weather and people were a hell of a lot nicer, (not like the lousy weather and jerks in Indiana). I loved Decatur and couldn't figure out why he felt that way.

Johnny was no fool; he had a plan. As soon as he graduated, he got a job as an apprentice brick mason. He worked hard and learned his trade. In a few short years, he became a full-fledged mason and now knew that he could find work anywhere. So he packed up his things and moved to California, land of milk and honey.

At first it must have been great. The beautiful beaches, the girls, the climate, and all of the new friends he was making. But as the months and years flew by and Johnny settled into a routine, he began to dislike a lot of Californians. He then noticed that they were no different than the dorks he had left back home in Indiana.

One morning, he woke up and realized that if he couldn't get along with the people in California, or the folks he knew in Indiana, maybe, just maybe, he was the problem. The more he thought about it, the more he realized that it must be him. All of those people couldn't be wrong! Facing the truth for the first time in his life, he became so depressed that he got out of bed, grabbed his pistol, and put an end to his misery.

The moral of this story is if you're not happy in Indiana, you won't be happy in California, Hawaii, or Timbuktu. Happiness has nothing to do with where you are geographically, but has everything to do with where you are mentally. Abe Lincoln said, "Most people are about as happy as they make up their minds to be."

When I was first married, I would get up in the morning, jump into the shower and sing my favorite Hank Williams and other country songs, beautifully I might add, while playing my air guitar. Then I would stand in front of the mirror, looking at my reflection admiringly, and tell myself what a handsome dog I was. After a few days, my wife, still not believing this daily ritual, said, "What's the matter with you? Are you nuts?"

"No," I explained, "I could get up and say, 'What a crummy day, I hate my lousy job, and look,' as I glanced into the mirror and pointed at my face, 'Another wrinkle!' I could go on complaining, but all it would do is make me feel awful even before I left the house. I don't want to feel awful. I want to feel great! Giving myself positive strokes and singing each morning makes me feel fantastic! I can control how I feel by how I think. It's my choice! So you see, you can choose to be happy or you can choose to be unhappy. Isn't it great to know that your happiness is up to you?"

Of course, no one can be happy all the time. I had an aunt who lived in Chicago, and they used to say that she wasn't quite right in the head. Why? Because no matter what anyone said or what happened, she would always laugh.

We're not supposed to be happy all the time. If we were, they'd probably confine us. Life has its ups and downs. Bad things happen to everyone, and when they do, we have a choice. We can choose to wallow in self-pity, or we can choose to get on with our lives, determined not to let these things get us down. It's not what happens to us that counts…it's how we handle it. Again, it's our choice!

Don't Let Them Pay

If someone else pays for your mistakes,

you're not going to learn much!

A Hairy Situation

I once owned a really neat restaurant and club called "The Paradise Café." A friend I hadn't seen for a few years dropped in and recognized me. He came over and said, "Hi, Jimmie, remember me?"

"Sure, Dave," I said. "How ya doing?"

"Great," he replied, as he looked me over.

"Boy," he continued, "You're sure losing your hair!"

"You want to see hair?" I quipped as I started to unbuckle my belt.

She Knows!

One day, I forgot what my wife Fry had wanted me to get for her.

In sheer frustration, she quipped, "Thank God your memory is the shortest thing on you!"

Toot Toot

Sometimes, if you don't toot your horn,

nobody will know you're around.

And sometimes if you do, nobody wants you around!

That's Italian?

I've developed a new Italian dish. It's a combination

of pizza and lasagna. It's called pizzanga.

Respect

Respect is an elusive thing. You can't demand it, you can't buy it

and no one can give it to you. You have to get it

the old-fashioned way…you must earn it! I guarantee that if

you treat everyone with fairness, honesty, sincerity, and dignity,

you will not only have their respect, you will have earned it!

Self-Discipline

Over thirty-five years ago, I had a great little pizza restaurant called Jimmie's Pizza. A regular customer of mine was a very wealthy man of obvious good taste, by the name of Phil Crawford. After work one evening, Phil asked me to join him for a drink. I jumped at the chance, because I always tried to find out what made people successful, in the hopes that it would rub off on me. It wasn't long before I steered the conversation around to just that.

"Phil," I asked, "Can you tell me why some people succeed and others don't?"

"I can't tell you everything that goes into making someone successful, but I can tell you the main reason why most people fail."

"Why's that?" I asked.

"Lack of self-discipline," he replied.

"Self-discipline?"

"Yeah," he went on. "It takes a lot of self-discipline to do the things you know will help you succeed, and to avoid the things that will pull you down or destroy you. It takes self-discipline to rise every morning, get to work on time and do the best job that you can possibly do. It takes self-discipline to sit down and write out your goals and plans for success. It takes self-discipline to constantly strive to improve yourself and learn more about your profession. It takes self-discipline to practice moderation in all things. Finally, it takes self-discipline to avoid drugs, for they will not only take your money; worse yet, they'll take your spirit.

"Wow, you make it sound like lack of self-discipline is the reason for all failure."

"If you were listening closely, you will have noticed that I said that it was the main reason. Of course, there are other reasons people fail. Lack of desire, determination, or preparation, to name a few."

"What about intelligence?" I wanted to know.

He continued, "Anyone with average intelligence can accomplish anything they want to and be a huge success, if they have the self-discipline, the desire, the determination, and prepare themselves. Even the dumbest kid in the class will pass, if he does his homework! The person with these qualities will go much farther in life than the so-called brains. It might be interesting to know how many of the truly successful people are Phi Beta Kappas or belong to the Mensa Society. I have no idea, but I'll bet damn few. You don't have to be an egghead or an intellectual giant to succeed!"

Boy, was I happy to hear that!

After some more small talk, our glasses were empty, and I gladly picked up the tab. In one short hour, I figured that I had gotten the equivalent of a college degree in success…and for just four dollars and sixty-five cents…plus tax!

No Know

Many people think that it's not what you know,

it's who you know that counts.

If they knew they wouldn't think that, because they'd be only half

right.

Without the ability to apply it, influence and clout are of little value.

Quoting Willie

"To be, or not to be?"

Now that's a real honey!

God, I hope I didn't bumble that!

Nor a Butterfly

In my lifetime, I've met many Millers,

But I've never met a Moth!

From Miller to Pillar

I've seen but never met a moth in my time,

I've been introduced to many a Miller.

And meeting the Post was simply divine,

But it hurt when I ran into the pillar!

Good-bye, Harold

I once had an attorney who thought he was more important than his client(s). This was obvious because he would seldom, if ever, return my calls. One frustrating day, after several unanswered ones, I got his secretary on the line.

"Susan?"

"Yes."

"This is Jim Schindler again. I need to talk to Harold."

"I'm sorry, he's on the phone."

"Well, you tell him that if he doesn't return my damn call, I'm going to get a new lawyer!"

"Okaaay, I'll tell him."

I no sooner hung up, when the phone rang. Picking it up, I answered, "Harold?"

"How'd you know?"

"Lucky guess," I replied.

Harold doesn't work for me anymore, and to this day I wonder if he has figured out why clients aren't flocking to his door.

Used To

After several unreturned calls to Mike, my CPA, I finally got a hold of him.

"Mike," I said, "did I ever tell you the story about the attorney who used to work for me?"

"No, I don't think so."

"He wouldn't return my calls!"

Enlightening

I knew a guy who was so religious

that when he read the passage,

"Let there be light," he got lit!

A Married Ham

I had just returned from a trip to Germany, and on my first day back in the office, Jim Horton, our Lima store manager, walked in.

"Hi, Jim," I greeted him.

"Hey, it's good to see you're back. Did you have a nice time?" he asked.

"Yeah, it was great."

"Did you pick up any German?"

"Jim, please," I replied, "I'm a married man!"

Missing What?

I think that it was at least twenty years ago that a friend of mine, Jimmy D'Angelo said, "Jimmie, do you play golf?"

"No," I replied.

"You don't know what you're missing!" he said.

Later on, I got to thinking about that and I came to this conclusion. If you don't know what you're missing...you're not missing it!

Shirtainly

I usually dress casually, khaki pants and a golf shirt with the name of my company, Bandido's, embroidered on it. A friend asked me, "Why do you always wear a Bandido's shirt?"

"Why should I wear a Tommy Middlefinger or an Abercrummy and Bitch shirt?" I replied. "Doesn't it seem logical that if I'm going to advertise a product, it ought to be my own?"

No Ties

Another friend once said, "Jim, you ought to wear a suit, or coat and tie to work."

"Why should I do that?" I asked.

"You'd look more professional and get more respect," he replied.

"If I'm so shallow that the only way I can get respect is by wearing a shirt and tie, then I don't deserve it."

He's Still #1

Mr. Welch, a high school teacher, was chewing out one of his students for something he had done. When he finished, he started to walk back to his classroom. After taking a couple of steps, he thought of something else he wanted to say, and turned around just in time to catch the irate underclassman flipping him the bird. "Oh," Mr. Welch said, "I'm glad to see that I'm still number one in your book!"

She's #1

I've been married twice, and my second wife's name is Fry. One day, not thinking or intending any harm, I referred to her as number two. As soon as I said it and glanced at the expression on her face, I knew I had made a major boo boo. Quickly, I looked at her and said as sweetly and convincingly as I could, "Honey, even though you're number two, you're number one in my heart!"

She Likes Me?

I often stop at fast food places when I'm on the road because it's convenient and, generally speaking, the rest rooms are reasonably clean. However, I feel a little guilty using their facility if I don't buy something, so I generally do.

This afternoon, the urge hit me so I whipped into a Burger King. After taking care of business, I went to the counter and ordered a large diet Coke.

"That'll be one dollar and thirty five cents," the gal said.

"A dollar thirty-five," I repeated. "I thought you liked me!"

"I do, they pay me to like all the customers."

"Oh, so does that mean you like me even if you don't?"

The American Depository

If all of the McDonalds in the United States closed,

there would be a national emergency.

Not because we couldn't find a place to eat,

but where would we go to the bathroom?

I can only surmise that there have been more deposits

made at Mickey D's than at the Bank of America!

Sinless Joe

A long time ago - the passing years have dimmed my recollection of the exact date, but it must have been about 1956 - my brother Joe was anxiously waiting for me to finish getting ready so we could to go to town.

"Come on, come on," he said, somewhat annoyed, "Let's get going!"

"Don't you know that patience is a virtue?" I responded.

"Sure," he answered, "but impatience is no sin."

Tall Hog

No matter how big or small you are,

if you're the only hog at the trough, you're tall hog!

A Brainy Observation

If God gave everyone a brain, why do so many people seem

brainless?

Fishermen

Fishermen have to be the most positive people on the planet. No matter how bad their luck, they enthusiastically approach each new day of angling with great expectations. If they tackled life with the same optimism, perhaps they would never again come up empty-handed!

Keep it to Yourself

If one person knows it...it's a secret.

If two people know it...it's not.

If three or more know it...it's common knowledge!

Ne'er-do-well

It's almost impossible to be good at something you don't like to do.

Stop... Stop!

In 1969, the building next door to the School Sisters of Notre Dame's convent was being remodeled. Sister Marie could barely hear the phone ringing above the construction noise.

"Hello, School Sisters of Notre Dame," she answered.

"Did anybody there order a hard-on?" a male voice asked.

Sister, being very devout but more naïve, said, "I don't know." Then thinking that it might be something for the construction next door, she asked, "What size?"

"Two by seven inches."

"Oh, let me ask the sisters."

Putting the receiver down, she walked over to the hallway and yelled, "Did anyone order a hard-on?"

A sister walking by gave her a what-in-heaven's-name-are-you-talking-about look, shrugged her shoulders and said, "No."

"I'm sorry, no one here ordered it," Sister Marie said politely into the phone.

The following Sunday, Father Bob, the parish priest, invited the sisters over for dinner. After some idle chitchat, Sister Marie said, "This week, I had the strangest phone call. A nice man called and asked if anyone ordered a hard-on."

The pious parish priest, holding up his hand like a traffic cop, shouted emphatically, "Stop... stop."

Then, the embarrassed sister finally realized that something was amiss. Returning to the convent that evening, she made a beeline to the study and found a dusty book on sex education. In a moment, there it was... the explanation.

"Oh, my!"

This incident had absolutely no bearing on Sister Marie's decision to leave the convent shortly thereafter. However, in 1999, thirty years later, she had some of the same sisters over for dinner. They still didn't know what the term meant! Marie explained.

"Oh, my!"

Sinsense

Sister Marie caught one of her grade school students lying, and she made her stay after school as punishment. The very next day, her mother came in to complain about the treatment of her daughter.

"Why did you keep my daughter after school?" she asked in a huff.

"Because I caught her lying."

"My daughter wouldn't lie. I taught her to always tell the truth," replied the upset parent.

"Yes, and my mother taught me not to sin," answered Sister Marie.

Gray is Good!

My wife Fry asked if it bothered me that my hair was turning gray.

"No," I answered. "I don't care what color it is, as long as I've still got some! Besides, I never fight the inevitable."

Grocery Lines

These days, it takes longer to pay for your
food at the grocery than it does to cook it!

At the grocery I found instantly,
Bacon, fresh eggs and green tea.
But to my dismay,
When I went to pay,
Last place in the slow line was me!

Doug, Cathy, and Bruce

My friend Doug divorced his wife, Cathy, and a short time later, came out of the closet and told his family and friends that he was gay. He now lives with his friend and companion, Bruce. About a month ago, my seventeen-year-old daughter Heidi and I went over to Doug's house to look at a commercial that he was working on for Bandido's, our restaurants. While we were viewing it, I said, "Fry [my wife's name], look at that."

"I'm Heidi," answered my daughter, somewhat irritated.

A little later, concentrating on the TV monitor, I said, "Rachel [my youngest daughter's name], isn't that neat?"

"Dad, I'm Heidi," she replied again. It was clear from the tone of her voice that she was becoming very annoyed.

Doug picked up on this, and trying to smooth things over said, "Heidi, if you think that's bad, you should have heard Bruce the night I called him Cathy!"

Turn up the Volume

Dr. Goldstein, who happens to be Jewish and undoubtedly one of the finest proctologists anywhere, decided that I needed a colonoscopy. The date was set: August 22, 2000, my birthday. A colonoscopy is a procedure where the doctor snakes a flexible rod with a light on the end of it, up through your large bowel to see if everything is okay.

While I was in the holding area being prepped for the procedure, Dr. Goldstein stopped by. "Do you know what my name is?" I asked him. Since he knows me pretty well, he gave me a puzzled look, and I then said, "Schindler, Doc, Schindler. Remember, I'm one of the good guys."

A few minutes later, as I lay in the operating room, waiting for them to start the anesthetic, I said to Dr. Goldstein, "Doc, when you have my intestines all lit up, would you sing 'Happy Birthday' to me? I'm sixty-six today."

I didn't recall much after that, since the anesthetic quickly took effect. However, when I came to, the nurse informed me that they did indeed sing "Happy Birthday" during the procedure.

"You're kidding?" I asked.

"We sure did. Even Dr. Goldstein sang. In fact, we asked him if he wanted us to get him a microphone."

"Well, he should have sung louder," I replied, "I didn't hear a damn thing."

Where You Sit Is Where You Stand!

At most business and social events,

where you sit says a lot about where you stand.

A Simple Business Plan

Many retail businesses seemingly look for excuses to close: i.e., holidays, bad weather (real or perceived), a family crisis, temporary power outages, etc. We look for reasons to stay open. We have never yet done a nickel's worth of business with our doors locked!

Rule # 1: If you want to do business, unlock the doors! There are only three exceptions to this rule. We never open on Easter, Thanksgiving, or Christmas. These are traditional family holidays, and I've yet to meet a boss or an owner who wanted to work them.

Rule # 2: Don't ask anyone to do what you're not willing to do!

The Route to Accomplishment

There are those that believe that if you want to get something done, you must do it a certain way (usually their way), and if you don't they become very upset.

A wise person knows that there is generally more than one way to accomplish something. Does it really matter which route we take as long as we reach our desired destination?

No Foolin'

I may no longer be young, but I'm still foolish!

And even tho' I'm growing out, I refuse to grow up!

She's Still Here!

A magician came into Bandido's Mexican Restaurant one day, and asked if I would employ him to entertain our guests.

"I'll tell you what," I said. "If you can do this one trick, I'll hire you."

"What's that?" he asked.

"Make my first wife disappear!"

50

Keep on Truckin'!

I drove down to Decatur for breakfast with a few of my old buddies at Two Brother's, a local pub. Tom Hurst, Jo-Jo Jauregui and Gene Hill showed up. During our conversation, Gene commented that he was looking for a pick-up truck.

"I thought you had one," I said.

"Yeah," he answered, "but it's a piece of crap."

"I thought that you were trying to sell it," Tom interjected.

"Until I worked on it," Gene cleverly added.

Indefenceable

My son John was three years old and his sister, Dawn, five. We had just moved into town, and I was concerned that John might run into the street, so I hired a company to put a four-foot chain link fence around the back yard.

A couple of weeks later, when I came home from work, they had the fence about finished. As I walked into the house, Dawn said, "What are they doing, Daddy?"

"They're putting up a fence to keep John in the back yard, so he won't go into the street and get run over," I answered.

"That's not going to stop John," she said, like she knew what she was talking about.

In an hour or so they had finished the fence, cleaned up their mess, and left. I then let the kids into the back yard to check it out and to watch John's reaction. He took one look at the fence, ran up to it and in less than ten seconds, climbed over it.

It isn't every day that you get outsmarted by a five-year-old!

PS: The little rascal never did get run over!

How Sweet It Ain't

Shortly thereafter, I bought the kids a sandbox. It just so happened that when I came home with bags of white sand to fill it with, John was taking a nap. When he got up and went into the back yard, it took him just a few seconds to notice the white granules glistening in the sun. He excitedly ran over to the sandbox, grabbed a handful and crammed it into his mouth. In a second or two, it was obvious by the look on his face and the white stuff spewing from his lips that he had figured out it wasn't sugar.

Bedtime Stories

Some of my fondest memories are of putting my kids to bed. I remember tucking in my daughter Jamie, and telling her bedtime stories. She would then say her prayers, and after that, we would sing a little song that I taught her. (Her nickname was Mimi, because when she was very little she couldn't pronounce Jamie, and that's what she called herself). I would sing, "Me…Me…Me…Me, Me, Me, Me." Then she would sing in the same tune, "Loves her daddy more than life itself." Next, we would always laugh, and I would give her a big hug and kiss good night. I think that her dad needed that as much as she did!

With my younger daughters, Heidi and Rachel, I started out reading "The Three Bears" and the other standard nursery rhymes, but as they grew older, they seemed to tire of them. So I began to make up stories about beautiful princesses, wicked monsters, evil villains, and handsome heroes. I would raise and lower my voice very dramatically. Sometimes, during a sad part, I'd even pretend to cry. By observing the expression in their eyes and on their cute little faces, I could watch their emotions ebb and flow with the story. Once I started to tell these fanciful yarns, that was the end of the fairy tales.

Their all-time favorite, though, was the poem "I know an old lady that swallowed a fly." They tried to get me to tell it every night, which I usually did. When I got to the part that went,

"I know an old lady that swallowed a spider,

That wiggled and jiggled and tickled inside her,"

I would tickle their tummies. They would pull the cover over their heads, screaming with laughter, just daring me to tickle them. If I didn't, they would pull down the covers and stick out their bellies, so I could then tickle them.

When the stories had been told and the tummies tickled, it was again time for prayers and goodnight hugs and kisses. For us, this was a perfect ending to our day! I hope that they remember this as fondly as I do.

I have no idea where or when I first heard that poem. I checked with the library and they told me that it was an old American folk tale (author unknown). There are several different versions, because it was spread by word of mouth. So, if any of you parents would like to use it, this is the way that I told it to my kids. Don't forget to tickle when you say, "wiggled and jiggled and tickled inside her."

"The Old Lady That Swallowed a Fly"
I know an old lady that swallowed a fly,
I don't know why she swallowed a fly,
Perhaps she'll die.

I know an old lady that swallowed a spider,
That wiggled and jiggled and tickled inside her.
She swallowed the spider to catch the fly,
I don't know why she swallowed the fly,
Perhaps she'll die.

I know an old lady that swallowed a bird.
How absurd to swallow a bird!
She swallowed the bird to catch the spider,
That wiggled and jiggled and tickled inside her.
She swallowed the spider to catch the fly.
I don't know why she swallowed the fly,
Perhaps she'll die.

I know an old lady that swallowed a cat.
Imagine that, she swallowed a cat.
She swallowed the cat to catch the bird.

She swallowed the bird to catch the spider,

That wiggled and jiggled and tickled inside her.

She swallowed the spider to catch the fly.

I don't know she swallowed the fly,

Perhaps she'll die.

I know an old lady that swallowed a dog.

What a hog, to swallow a dog.

She swallowed the dog to catch the cat.

She swallowed the cat to catch the bird.

She swallowed the bird to catch the spider,

That wiggled and jiggled and tickled inside her.

She swallowed the spider to catch the fly.

I don't know why she swallowed the fly,

Perhaps she'll die.

I know an old lady that swallowed a goat.

She just opened her throat, and swallowed a goat!

She swallowed a goat to catch the dog.

She swallowed the dog to catch the cat.

She swallowed the cat to catch the bird.

She swallowed the bird to catch the spider,

That wiggled and jiggled and tickled inside her.

She swallowed the spider to catch the fly.

I don't know why she swallowed the fly,

Perhaps she'll die.

I know an old lady that swallowed a cow.

Can you imagine how she swallowed a cow?

She swallowed the cow to catch the goat.

She swallowed the goat to catch the dog.

She swallowed the dog to catch the cat.

She swallowed the cat to catch the bird.

She swallowed the bird to catch the spider,

That wiggled and jiggled and tickled inside her.

She swallowed the spider to catch the fly.

I don't know why she swallowed the fly,

Perhaps she'll die.

I know an old lady that swallowed a horse.

She's dead, of course!

Whatever Happened to Little Chuckie?

Several years ago, my wife Fry (who was called Rosanne when she was a kid) and I met two of our gay friends, Denny and Vic, for dinner. After we finished, they asked if we'd care to accompany them to "Up the Street," a gay bar. Since my wife and I had never been to one, we thought that it would be a new experience, and agreed.

As soon as we entered the bar, a very large person, (about two hundred and sixty pounds, and tall, about six foot two) in full make-up and a long dress, said, "That will be two dollars apiece...cover charge."

We paid, went in and took a seat right next to the dance floor.

"Fry," I said, "Either the person collecting the cover charge is a guy, or else that is the ugliest woman that I've ever seen!"

Soon, the floorshow started, and a very attractive lady sang and told jokes.

"She is really good," I commented.

"That's not a she, that's a man," Denny corrected me.

"No, it's not!" I argued.

"Yes, she is," Vic, Denny's friend, joined in.

"You're kidding?" I said, still not convinced.

"Well, she is," Vic went on. "Take our word for it...we know!"

I now believed them, but I still couldn't believe my eyes!

Later, when the show was over, we were talking and having a good time when the very large person in a full-length dress who had taken our cover charge approached our table. She stood right behind my wife, bent over, tapped her on the shoulder and said in this deep, masculine voice, "Rosanne...Rosanne, is that you?"

My wife, somewhat surprised and a little scared, turned around, looked at this immense individual, and said, "Yes...s...s...s."

"Don't you remember me?"

"No...o...o...o," she said, racking her brain.

"I'm little Chuckie," he exclaimed in this huge bass voice. "I used to live down the alley from you when we were kids!"

At that point, we all cracked up. I pounded on the table in a fit of hysteria, and laughed so hard that I slid right out of my chair...and under the table.

Let It Snow!

For the past several years, I've had a swollen prostate. My bladder would not empty completely, requiring many trips to the men's room. When I did go, I had a weak stream, or in lay terms, I'd just dribble...dribble. During the night, I'd have to get up an average of three to five time to go to the bathroom.

Dr. Schlueter, my urologist, decided that it was time to do something about it, so he recommended a transurethral resection of the prostate (TURP). Again in lay terms, a roto-rooter job.

Thank God, the surgery was a success. My bladder now empties completely, my stream is good, and I get up only once a night...sometimes not at all.

When we were kids on the farm, my brother Joe and I would have contests to see who could pee the farthest. It was always better if there was snow on the ground, because it was harder to cheat and a lot easier to tell who won. So now, with all my newfound pressure...I can't wait for it to snow!

Coming or Going?

I try to go for a walk around the golf course at Foster Park, here in Fort Wayne, every other day. I read sometime ago, that walking backwards was good for you, so I made it part of my routine.

As I was walking backwards, John Erb, a friend of mine who was golfing, spotted me and said, "Hey, Jimmie, what the heck are you doing?"

"You know me," I answered, "Half the time, I don't know if I'm coming or going!"

I'm Finished!

My kids, Jimmie and Heidi, and I went down to watch my daughter Jenny, run a 5K race at the Three Rivers Festival, in Fort Wayne. After wishing her good luck, I asked her where the race started. "Right here," she said, pointing at a line painted on the street.

"Where does it end?"

"The finish line is here, too," she replied.

"Oh," I said, "You're beginning at the end? Does that mean when you start...you're finished?"

No Gas

Jenny ran the 5K race in twenty-one minutes and fifty-three seconds. Not too bad! We then began to discuss various contestants and how long it had taken them to run the course. Finally, I said, "If I ran it, do you know what I'd run?"

"No," Jenny answered.

"Out of gas!"

Real Nuts

This morning, my son Jimmie and I met Doss Fisher, his sister, Norma, and some friends for breakfast. While we were eating, a men's softball team came in, pushed a few tables together next to us and sat down. They were having a good ol' time, when one of the players asked us, "Are you guys from here?"

"Yeah," someone responded.

"What's a Hoosier?" he asked somewhat sarcastically.

"A Hoosier is someone from Indiana," Doss answered.

"Where are you guys from?" I asked.

"We're from Ohio."

"What are you called?"

"We're Buckeyes."

I just couldn't resist. "What's a Buckeye?"

"A buckeye's a nut," one of them replied.

"Oh," I said, "Does that mean that you guys are a bunch of nuts?"

The Ultimate Relaxation

Henry Husmann was decorating a house for Dr. Mulligan, a dentist. Henry is very focused, and when he does a job, he works fast and hard. After a few days of observing him, Dr. Mulligan said, "Henry, you'd better let up a little and learn how to take it easy. Do you play golf?"

"No," said Henry, "I don't have the time."

"It's so relaxing," the good doctor went on. "You should take it up. Why don't you play a round with me tomorrow morning? You need to get away. I won't take no for an answer!"

Reluctantly, Henry agreed and the following morning they met at the scheduled time. "It's so beautiful and peaceful out here," Dr. Mulligan said as he teed up his ball. "Don't you feel better already?" Henry nodded in agreement, while thinking of all the work that he wanted to get done.

Dr. Mulligan was now in the process of swinging; he hit the ball and it started straight down the fairway, but quickly hooked so far to the left that it landed on the adjacent one. There was a brief silence, then some choice words, followed by a golf club flying through the air. The doctor was not a happy man, but by the time they had played a couple more holes, he had settled down.

Henry, not being a golfer, was content just to get the ball in the cup, and keep the game moving so he could get back to the job.

On the eighth hole, Dr. Mulligan had a six-foot putt for par. He took his time, lined up the ball, and tapped it a good three feet past the hole. It was apparent by the Doc's increasingly reddening face that his dander was getting up. He bent over his club, tried once more to drop the ball in, but all of the Irish Saints, including the good St. Bridget and St. Patrick, must have forsaken him, for the ball rimmed the cup and popped right out. Such a tirade will never be heard again on that golf course as spewed from the crimson face of our tooth puller. He threw his putter, ran over, picked it up and wrapped it around the nearest tree. Then he glanced at Henry and said in a huff, "You can keep on playing if you want to, but I'm quitting!"

On their walk back to the clubhouse, Henry said, "You shouldn't get so upset. It's only a game. You're going to have a heart attack out there if you keep that up."

"I don't give a damn," he replied, still annoyed.

It was no surprise to Henry when he found out a few years later that the genial doctor had had a heart attack and died while relaxing and playing golf in Florida.

A Win Win

Every time I've read or heard about a strike, the union was demanding either shorter hours, more benefits, or higher wages...if not all three. Not once have I ever heard or read about them pledging to work harder to help the company become more efficient and profitable, if the company met their demands. Wouldn't it be wonderful if they said something like, "I'll tell you what. If you give us more money and more benefits, we'll work harder, be more productive, and do a better job."

No company or enterprise can long survive if one side gives and gives, and the other side takes and takes. After a while there will be nothing left to give, and nothing left to take. Then both sides lose. The company loses its business and the workers lose their jobs. Only when the agreement benefits both management and labor will everyone win and continue to prosper.

Thank You, Jesus!

"Jim."

Silence.

"Jim."

More silence.

Much louder, "Jim…why don't you ever listen to me?"

Putting the morning paper down, Jim looked at his wife and said, "I was reading; I didn't hear you."

"You know, the first thing to go when you get old is your hearing," she said, somewhat irritated.

"Thank God!" he replied with a big grin.

Doe Talk

A buck is just a buck, but a big buck is better!

An Idiotic Question

If every village has one, why are there so many on the highways?

The Hole Story

Bruce was unhappily married for several years, and his wife was constantly criticizing and putting him down. She was notorious for her big mouth and it was rumored that she had the disposition of a wart hog that hadn't pigged out for many a day.

He had had just about all he could take, and was about to tell her that he was going to file for a divorce, when she told him that she was pregnant. He felt that there was no way he could leave her now.

Maybe, just maybe, with this turn of events, they could work things out. Besides, if he left her and the baby in a lurch, he could never forgive himself.

My observations have taught me that there are three kinds of pregnant women. The first type love their husbands and really want a child. You can tell it by their cheerful disposition, and they seem to have this wonderful sense of peace and serenity. They are the women that are truly beautiful pregnant.

The second kind didn't really want a child, but they become resigned to the inevitable, and make the best of the situation.

The third kind, for whatever reason, become miserable and want to make sure that everyone else around them is, too! Usually they succeed.

Unfortunately for Bruce, his wife fell into the third category. Still, he believed that it was his duty to stand by her during this period, even though her mouth got nastier and more insulting. She complained about everything from his manhood to his ability to support his family. He even attended Lamaze classes with her to help prepare for the birth. How he hung in there is beyond me.

Finally, the big day came. She was lying in the delivery room, Bruce holding her hand, coaching her while she screamed and told him what a no good son-of-a-bitch he was. After twenty minutes or so, the doctor said, "The baby is starting to crown. If you want to see it born, you better come down here."

Bruce went to the other end of the table and took a look. "My God," he said to himself, "I never thought that I'd ever see another hole on her as big as her mouth!"

Sour Doe

We've all heard the expression, "The buck stops here."

But do you really know what happens when the buck stops?

The doe gets mad!

A Famous Name

In nineteen fifty-one, I was seventeen and owned a 1936 green Chevy with bright yellow wheels. I was very proud of it, for it not only looked good...it ran! Besides, Adrian Baker and I were the only two kids in our class of thirty-six at Decatur Catholic High School that had cars.

With nothing better to do one night, several of my buddies and I were cruising the town, when I went around the corner at Thirteenth and Monroe St. pretty fast. In a few seconds, I heard a siren, glanced in my rear mirror and saw a state police car with lights a-flashing. I pulled over, rolled down my window, and waited for him.

"What were you doing going around that corner on two wheels?" he asked.

"I didn't go around it on two wheels," I lied.

"Don't tell me you didn't; I saw you!" he said angrily. "Let me see your driver's license."

I fumbled through my billfold and handed it to him. (I just knew that I was going to get a ticket). He studied it for a moment and said, "Is your name Schindler?"

"Yes, sir," I answered politely.

"Who are your parents?"

"My father was Louis," I replied, wondering why he wanted to know.

"Where's he from?"

"He was from Trinity, but he's dead now."

"My name is Walter Schindler. I'm from Berne, and I was just wondering if we were related," the officer responded.

We talked some more, and decided that we were not. By the time we finished our discussion, he had calmed down and I could tell that he felt better about me. He then handed my driver's license back to me and said, "You better take it easy, and don't let me catch you again."

"Yes, sir," I said gratefully.

My buddies were amazed that I didn't get a ticket. "Well, that's what happens when you've got a famous name," I boasted. (This was a long time before I ever heard of "Schindler's List.")

I knew that I was very fortunate because of the name coincidence. Without it I would almost certainly have been cited. When I told Officer Schindler that I hadn't gone around that corner on two wheels, what I really did was call him a liar. That night, I learned that arguing with, or lying to, a policeman is a sure way to get arrested or a ticket; unless of course, you have the same famous last name!

The Truth Works!

Many years later, I was driving to Decatur when I instinctively looked into my rear view mirror and saw a police car behind me with his lights flashing. No siren.

"Damn it," I said to myself, as I pulled over.

The officer approached my car and said, "May I see your driver's license and registration?"

"Yes, sir," I said politely and handed them to him.

He looked them over, and said, "I timed you doing sixty-five in a fifty-five zone."

"Oh hell," I blurted out, "I thought I was going faster than that!"

He gave me a surprised look, broke into a big smile, handed me back my papers and said, "Well, you better slow it down." He then got into his car, shut off his gotcha lights and left.

I can only speculate, but I think that I was probably the first person he'd ever stopped that admitted going faster than he was clocked, which was, to him, a refreshing change.

Definition:

Risqué: not as dirty as dirty.

Short Solution

A quick fix generally doesn't last long!

No Messed-Up Relations

One evening, my wife Fry and I were having a drink at Henry's Bar with a good friend of ours, William Eichhorn. We have been friends for many years, and he knew all about my being raised at St. Vincent's Villa, a Catholic orphanage. During our conversation, he told us of his upbringing, all the problems his family had had when he was a kid and the adverse effect they had on him. He also discussed some of his other friends, their dysfunctional families and the guilt, low self-image, and other baggage that they carry with them as a result, to this very day. Then without hesitation he said, "You don't know how lucky you were, being raised in an orphan's home."

No one had ever said that to me before, so I asked somewhat curiously, "What makes you say that?"

"Because," he continued, "you never had any parents to screw you up!"

A Relative Theory

Everything's relative...and I got too damn many of 'em!

Place the Blame on James

In nineteen sixty-two, I was going with a very attractive lady who had five children from her previous marriage. She was having an extremely tough time. Her ex had taken off, and was not paying one cent to help support the children. She held a full time job at the General Electric plant on the assembly line, but still needed welfare to make ends meet.

I was also struggling, doing drywall part time. However, being young and impetuous, we decided to get married. Almost without exception, all of my friends and family were against it. "If you marry her with all those kids," they unanimously informed me, "You'll never have a damn thing!"

"If I never have a damn thing," I replied, "It won't be because of those kids. It'll be because old Jim Schindler doesn't have what it takes!"

> "The fault, dear Brutus, is not in our stars,
>
> but in ourselves, that we are underlings."
>
> William Shakespeare

Small Talk

During the four years that I attended John Carroll University, I worked in the library. In the office there were four or five older ladies who took care of the administrative duties. They were all very nice and we got along famously. However, like many of their kind, they enjoyed wagging their tongues and talking about anyone and everyone on campus. No deed, rumor, or scandal was too large or small to escape their attention and commentaries.

I had finished working one evening, and went into the office to ask the ladies if they wanted me to do anything else before I clocked out.

"No," one of them replied, "I believe that takes care of everything."

"Okay, I think I'll leave then and give you ladies something to talk about," I said in half-jest. They all smiled, one laughed, but I knew that they just couldn't wait for me to go so they could get started!

No Rushin'

On the name tag of a host at Bandido's was Ivan.

"Ivan," I asked, "Are you Russian?"

"No, he replied, "I'm not even in a hurry."

Tom Terrific

In nineteen sixty-eight, I was getting ready to open my first pizza restaurant, and signed a lease with Tom Jehl, the shopping center developer. Our agreement said that he would finish the interior, stub out the electrical and plumbing, and I would be responsible for hooking up our equipment. Everything seemed to go on schedule, and in a few months the contractor told me that we could start to install the ovens, etc.

The first thing I noticed was that nothing had been done in the rest- rooms. "When are you going to finish them?" I inquired of Bill, the contractor.

"You have to install them," he informed me.

"That's not what we agreed to," I said, somewhat upset. (Quite frankly, I didn't have the money.)

"Well, you're going to have to talk to Tom, because all the other tenants did."

I left and went to the construction office, where I knew Tom would be.

"Tom," I blurted out, "Bill said that we have to finish the restrooms, and that's not what you told me!"

"Jim," Tom replied, "I talk to a lot of people and can't remember every single conversation. Now, exactly what did I say?"

"You told me that you'd finish everything, and all I'd have to do is install the equipment."

"Well, if that's what I told you, that's what I'll do." And he kept his word!

After we had been open awhile, it became apparent that the air conditioner was undersized and wouldn't keep the restaurant cool enough. The engineer obviously hadn't figured the heat from the ovens and other kitchen equipment into his calculations. Again I went to see Tom.

"Tom, it's hotter than hell in our kitchen. The air conditioner is too small to handle the load. I think your engineer screwed up."

"What do you want me to do?" he asked.

"The lease says that you will provide adequate heating and air conditioning," I replied, expecting an argument.

"I'll get someone over to take care of it," he said. And he did!

Tom proved that he was a man of integrity, and to this day I'd do a million dollar deal with him on just his word. As a matter of fact, Art Spriou, another successful and ethical businessman, told me this past week that he and Tom did a deal to build a theater complex and bowling alley on just a handshake. Wouldn't it be great if there was that kind of trust in every relationship?

Tom has not only earned my respect, but also the respect and admiration of everyone that worked with him. It was not by accident that he has become one of Fort Wayne's most successful and well-liked developers. To me he will always be "Tom Terrific."

The Rotten Apple

The reason so many old sayings have survived the test of time is because they contain much wisdom and truth. The following is just one example.

In bygone days, apples were stored in barrels. If there was a bad apple in there, it spoiled the surrounding ones, and so on. Consequently, there is an old saying dating from the 1300s that goes, "A rotten apple spoils the barrel."

There will be times during the course of your life that you will encounter people who are chronic complainers, are constantly stirring up trouble, and are a negative influence. Just like that rotten apple, they must be thrown out before they spoil everything they touch.

Big Bad Ben

If Ben Franklin, one of our founding fathers,
were alive today, he would probably be arrested
for advocating child abuse. After all, wasn't he
the guy who said, "Spare the rod and spoil the child"?

He Sees, But Does Not Hear!

This morning I had an appointment with my optometrist, Dr. Hockemeyer, who is not only good, but also very thorough. "Doc," I said, "I've got good and bad news."

"Give me the bad."

"Out of the corner of my right eye I see little flashes of light that look just like lightning, only they're about three inches long and straight."

"It sounds like you might have a detached retina. Let's take a look."

He dilated my eyes, and after an extensive examination, said, "Just as I thought: the fluid in your retina is detaching. There's a gel-like substance in the retina, and as it detaches, there is a small possibility that the retina might tear. If you see a lot more of that lightning or a bunch of floaters, give me a call. Otherwise there's nothing to worry about. It happens to almost everyone as they age."

"Unless I'm mistaken," I said, "my left eye is the same age as my right one, and I'm not having any trouble with it!"

"There's a good chance that you will. Now what is the good news?"

"The good news is, even though I see lightning, I don't hear any thunder!"

Boredom

Boredom dulls the wits,

and saps one's energy.

Lose Talk

A lot of people can talk a good
game, but not many can play one!

Never Strive

Never strive for perfection, because it's an unattainable goal,
and you'll just be frustrated. Instead, try to constantly
improve yourself, and be the best that you can possibly be.

Grandpa Didn't Monkey Around!

If you want to believe that your great, great, great, great, great, great,
great, great, etc., grandfather was an ape, go ahead. *Mine wasn't!*

Here, Kitty, Kitty

In 1953, I was attending John Carroll University and living at
Bernet Hall, in a four-man room. Fr. Millor, a Jesuit priest, was the
dorm prefect. He had a gruff manner, and it surprised me that no one
had figured out that he was actually a softy.

Now college kids aren't noted for being neat and tidy, and
most of the time our room was pretty much what you'd expect of four
teenagers living together. Even Fr. Millor was appalled one evening at
the mess he saw when he walked into our room.

"I want this place cleaned up before you guys go out tonight.
This room is a sty," he exclaimed. "If you're a pig, you live in a pig
sty; if you're a cow you live in a barn; and if you're a dog, you live in
a dog house."

"Father," I said, "what if you're a cat?"

"Well," he answered with a twinkle in his eye, "I guess you'd live in a cat house."

No Use

Fr. O'Brien was the second floor prefect at Bernet Hall. One evening, a few of us were sitting around in his office chewing the fat, when Gene Riegelsberger, who was about to be married, said, "Father, my fiancée wants to buy a double bed. I have a hard time sleeping with anyone, so I would rather get two single beds. We're having a little argument over this. What do you think that we should do?"

The pious priest then prophesized, "For the first year or so, you're only going to use one, anyway… buy a double!"

Let's Take a Look!

My sister Margie recently went to visit her husband's grave. Her daughter, Gayle, and her four-year-old granddaughter, Maggie, went along. When they got to the cemetery, Maggie wanted to know what they were doing. They explained that they had come to visit Grandpa, who had died and was buried there.

"Where?" Maggie asked.

"Right down there, in the ground," her mother answered.

Excitedly, she exclaimed, "Let's dig him up – I wanna see him!"

Nuts To You

Recently I was introduced to David Childers, a sales representative from Acorn Restaurant Supply. "Working for Acorn," I said. "You should be called Mr. Oak."

He pulled out his business card that had a picture of two acorns on it, threw it onto the table and said, "Here's a couple of nuts for you."

"I have a couple, too," I replied, "but I don't put them on the table!"

We Got His Goat

In Mexico City, there is a restaurante that specializes in cabrito (baby goat). I can't remember its Spanish name, but translated it means the Post Office. Jesus de la Rosa, our Mexican driver and guide, took us there for dinner. I like to try new things, so I ordered it (goat). I thought that it was a little greasy, but I liked it. (And no, it didn't taste like chicken!). As we were leaving, the owner asked us how everything was.

"Don't worry," I answered, "We'll be baaaaaak!"

Emergency Pick-up

My wife Fry and I were sitting at a red light, when we noticed a fire engine coming toward us with lights flashing and siren blaring. It barreled through the red light and as soon as it had gone by, it made a left-hand turn behind us, into the Pizza Hut. The driver then turned off the siren and emergency lights. Fry watched all this, and then turned to me and casually commented, "Wouldn't it be cheaper to have it delivered?"

Nasty Ole Flies

"Don't you just hate flies without zippers?"

"Yeah, but I hate it worse when time flies!"

I Feel Terrific

"Jim, how ya feeling?"

"Well, the last time I felt myself, I felt terrific!"

I'm Selling Me

The other day, I struck up a conversation with a stranger while waiting at the dentist office. We discussed the weather, the upcoming Notre Dame football season, and made other small talk. Wanting for something else to talk about, I asked, "What do you do?"

"I'm a salesman," he answered.

"What's your line?" I wanted to know.

"I sell me!" he replied enthusiastically.

"You sell what?" I said, puzzled by his answer.

"Me."

"Me? What do you mean me?"

"Most sales people think they sell a product or service," he went on, "but if they are truly successful, they understand that the first thing they must sell is themselves."

"Themselves?"

"Yes, did you ever buy anything from someone that you didn't like or trust?"

"No," I had to admit.

"Most people don't," he continued. "So the first thing a salesman must do is to sell himself. He must be polite, sincere and honest. If you're phony it can generally be detected or sensed, and you won't gain your client's confidence or trust. Stated simply, if your clientele doesn't like or have faith in you, you won't make the sale, and I don't give a damn how good your product is."

"Are you trying to tell me that all successful salesmen are honest and sincere?"

"Of course I am," he answered emphatically. "Sure, dishonest and deceitful people sell everything from airplanes to zippers, but they don't last long before it catches up with them. Then they are forced to move from job to job, or town to town, one step in front of upset clients or the law. I wouldn't call them successful."

"So, all you have to do to be a super salesman is to sell yourself?"

"You will note that I said the first thing you must do is to sell yourself. Of course there are other factors. You must know and believe in your product, and you must sincerely want to give your customers the best possible deal. It is also self-evident that the more customers you call on, the more you'll sell. However, at the risk of being repetitive, I want to emphasize that the first and most important thing you must do is to sell yourself."

"Well, I think you're right," I commented.

"You do?"

"Yeah, you just sold me!"

Family Matters

Recently my friend Norman Meyers turned seventy. Last night, he took my wife and I out for dinner at Peppercorn's. I always enjoy his company because he is truly "The Universal Man." He was born in Switzerland, and was raised and educated in England. Besides the United States, he has also lived in Italy and Canada. Moreover, he speaks four languages.

As a very successful businessman, he has traveled all over the world and met many of its leaders, among them Anwar Sadat; King Hussein of Jordan; King Faisal of Saudi Arabia; Helmut Schmidt, Chancellor of Germany; and Pope John XXIII.

He own homes in Canada, England, Texas, Florida, and here in Fort Wayne, IN.

It is obvious that he is well-educated, well-traveled, well-connected and successful. During our conversation last night, I asked him this question. "Norman, I'm sure that you have many great years still ahead of you, but if you had to live your life over, what would you do differently?"

Without hesitation, he replied, "I'd spend more time with my family...with my kids. The most important thing in life is your family. It's the only thing that really counts!"

Isn't it a shame that many people don't realize this until it's too late? We are so busy running around, making a living, and doing whatever, that we often ignore what is dearest to us, our families.

The only ones that stood by and supported me in good times and bad were my family. When I was going through a tough time and almost lost everything, many of my so-called friends were nowhere to be found. Some of them I had known and done business with for over twenty years. We went out together, attended each other's children's weddings, and so forth. But when the chips were down, they took off like the proverbial rats deserting the sinking ship. On the other hand, without exception, my family gave me their support and encouragement. I couldn't have made it through those times without them.

I found out the hard way that our families are probably the only ones that will stick with us, good or bad, throughout our entire lives. They, the people who support and love us the most, are the very ones we oft-times treat the worse. I can only surmise that if we treated our friends that way, we wouldn't have any!

Sometimes, when I see older folks giving all that attention to and making over their pets, I wonder if they treated their kids half that well. If they did, I bet they have great kids. If they didn't, could that be why their relationship with their children is strained or non-existent?

Since, as Norman Meyers said, "The most important thing in life is your family," doesn't it make sense to treat them at least as well as you would your best friend… or perhaps even better?

A Cut Above

You don't have to be on the cutting edge

to lead the pack, but you have to be pretty sharp!

Think Deep

I once stopped by a farm to buy some fresh tomatoes and roasting ears. The farmer, his son and daughter were working the roadside stand. I noticed what nice-looking kids he had, and said, "You sure have beautiful children."

"Thanks," he said. "Do you want to know how to have good-looking kids?"

"Sure," I replied, not knowing what to expect.

"Being a farmer," he continued, "I found out that if you want a terrific crop, you have to plant the seed deep!"

It Didn't Dawn on Me!

My daughter Dawn was about twelve years old when I said, "Dawn, we are going to have to have a little talk about the birds and bees."

"You mean about sex?" she asked.

"Yeah."

"Okay, Dad, what do you want to know?"

Eric Speaks the Truth

It was my birthday and my family took me out to dinner. During our meal, Eric, my-son-in-law, asked, "How old are you?"

"Sixty-five," I answered.

"Boy, you sure look good for your age!"

"You're just saying that because it's true," I quipped.

Which One?

In 1961, my sisters Bancy and Mouse took my sixty-three year-old mother on a trip out West. In a few days, they found themselves in Amarillo, Texas, and decided to get something to eat. They pulled up to a roadhouse, went in and ordered breakfast.

While they were waiting for their food, Bancy went to the jukebox and played a few tunes. Mom really liked Nat King Cole, so she played one of his songs for her.

During this time, Mom was looking out the window, watching three Mexicans who had just gotten out of a red pick-up, and were now coming into the restaurant.

Bancy sat down, and said, "Mom, there's Nat King Cole," meaning his song was starting to play.

"Which one, which one?" Mom asked, staring at the Mexicans.

Hi, Mom

Last Father's Day, one of my friends said,

"You know for a father, you're a real mother!"

Sittin's Bull

I broke my neck in 1956. Fortunately, my spinal cord wasn't injured and there was no paralysis. I wore a full body cast with just my face and arms sticking out. They cut a hole where my stomach was, for expansion, and a hole on top of my head for ventilation. Where I sat down, the cast would rest on the top of my thighs.

I wore that damn thing for three months, and when they removed it, I had to wear a brace that held my head immobile, for at least another six months. Overall, I couldn't work, play, or do anything strenuous for almost two years.

I was twenty-two years old, and in spite of my neck, I was full of piss 'n' vinegar and felt great. However, lying around with no outlet for all that stored-up energy made me a nervous wreck. The palms of my hands broke out, I felt tense and at times just wanted to scream or kick in the wall. The doctor said, "It's just nerves." Nevertheless, this experience taught me a valuable lesson. Sitting around with nothing to do is not only boring, it'll drive you nuts!

Recently, a friend of mine said, "I just can't wait to retire."

"What are you going to do, when you do?" I asked.

"Oh, I'm just going to relax, sit on the beach, and take it easy."

"I broke my neck once," I explained, "And for almost two years, I couldn't do a damn thing except sit on my butt. So let me tell you, sitting around on your ass ain't what it's cracked up to be!"

Gracias Garcia

In nineteen eighty-four, Don Kreamelmeyer and I were in Mexico City, buying artifacts to decorate a new Bandido's restaurant that I was about to open. After a long day of shopping, Jesus de la Rosa, our guide, took us to a very nice place to eat. We ordered drinks and when the waiter brought them over, trying to be funny I said, "Garcia."

Now we all know that Garcia is a name, and gracias means thank you. So when I said "Garcia" to the waiter, he looked at me, put his hand in front of his mouth to hide his laughter, and headed for the kitchen. Later on, he brought our food, and when he set it down, I again said, "Garcia."

"No, no," he said, wagging his finger back and forth at me. "No Garcia, senor…gracias, gracias."

Nodding my head in mock agreement, I responded, "Gracias, Garcia."

"No, no, no," he exclaimed in frustration, pointing to himself, "No Garcia, no Garcia."

"Oh," I replied, "Garcia, Senor Gracias."

With that, he threw back his head, rolled his eyes, and took off pronto for the kitchen, never again to set eyes on this crazy gringo!

Tim's Hot!

Tim really enjoyed going to Vegas and testing his gambling skills against the casinos. He was quite a character, and a classic example of the phrase, "Hope springs eternal in the sucker's breast."

Even though he inevitably came home with empty pockets, he honestly believed that he'd clean up on his next trip to the neon city.

On his latest spree, he was brimming with confidence, but into the third day of his five-day stay, he was broke. So, he picked up the phone, dialed his wife at home and enthusiastically exclaimed, "Honey, send me five thousand dollars; I'm on a hot streak!"

A Cheap Thrill at Kroger's

I very seldom go grocery shopping, but one day I found myself in a supermarket walking down the aisle, intently looking for some chili powder. As I reached the end of the aisle, I turned the corner, not paying attention to anything except what was on the shelves, and ran head-on into this buxom woman. I bounced back about a foot or so, took one look at her and said, "Nice running into you!"

Her smile was as big as her God-given assets!

A Cruel Cut

Dennis owned quarter horses. How he loved to ride and work with them! Even though he was from Indiana, he pictured himself as a macho cowboy. Recently, he took his wife and horses on a camping and riding trip to the Ozarks.

The campground was pretty rustic, but had a common facility with rest rooms, showers, and lavatories. One evening, after a hard day of riding in the bush, he headed for the men's room to clean up.

On returning to his campsite, he was madder than a yellow jacket trapped in a bottle.

"What's the matter with you?" his wife asked.

"Don't you ever buy me one of those throw-away razors again!" he shouted angrily at her.

"Why?" she said, somewhat puzzled.

"You just won't believe how embarrassed I was!"

"Embarrassed?"

"Yeah. I was shaving with that damn pink Bic throw-away razor you bought me, when in walked this guy and started to shave at the sink right next to me...with his bowie knife!"

The Appraisal

In the 1960s, I&M (Indiana and Michigan Electric Co.), wanted to run a power line across several farms north of town. The farmers got together and were very upset because they believed that they would not get a good price for their land. A meeting was then set up with I&M.

An executive from the power company made a hurried call to Tom Jehl, a local developer, who was well-respected and knowledgeable about the land values in that area.

"Tom," he said, "I wonder if you would appraise the farms that we want to run our power lines across and come up with a price that would be fair to all?"

"Sure, I can do that," Tom replied.

"There's only one catch: it's an emergency. We need it for a meeting with the farmers Friday."

"That doesn't give me much time, but I'll see what I can do."

Tom got all the necessary information, drove out to inspect the proposed right-of-way, wrote his report and dropped it off, along with his bill, at I&M.

Within an hour or so, he received a phone call from them. "Tom, how can you justify an eight hundred dollar fee, when it couldn't have taken more than a few hours?"

"I'll tell you what, I'll send you another invoice and break it down for you," Tom said.

He then sent the following statement.

Visiting the proposed right away and farms: $100.00

Knowing what to do when I got there: $700.00

Total Amt. Due: $800.00

The bill was promptly paid in full!

It Was Great!

"Man, I can sure tell I'm getting old!"

"You can?"

"Yeah, I saw a re-run of the Lawrence Welk show on TV the other night...and I really enjoyed it!"

Surprise Package

I was walking around our restaurant, Bandido's, talking to customers, doing a little PR, when I stopped at a table occupied by a middle-aged couple.

"Hi, folks, are they taking good care of you?" I asked.

"Yes, everything is great."

I then noticed that the gentleman had only finished about half of his meal, and it was obvious that he was finished eating.

"Was your dinner okay?"

"It was delicious, but I ate too much chips and sauce."

"Well, you better clean up your plate," I kidded. "Don't you know that there are people starving in China?"

"Here," he said, as he handed me his plate, "Mail it to them!"

Just Another Pretty Face

In the early 1970s, my wife and I went to a convention in San Francisco. After the meetings one afternoon, we took a walk, saw this nice little bar, and decided to go in for a drink. We sat there for a few minutes, relaxing and enjoying our cocktails, when my wife suddenly remarked, "Do you notice anything?"

I looked around curiously, and said, "No, why?"

"Well, it really upsets me," she exclaimed.

"What?" I wanted to know.

"All the guys in here are looking at you!"

Boy, I felt like just another pretty face!

Self-Image

The most important thing that you can give your children,

to ensure their success in life, is a good self-image.

This can easily be done through encouragement,

praise and unconditional love.

Who'd-a Thunk It!

Build a better mousetrap, and you'll catch more mice!

The Easy Way

The path most traveled is the path of least resistance.

Thanks, Doc

I opened our second restaurant in 1970. Although we had a manager in each unit, I worked the day shift in one store, and the night shift in the other. Worse yet, I wouldn't let the managers do their jobs. I constantly interfered with their decisions, and felt that no one could do it as well as I could.

After a few months, I started to get chest pains and decided to get a check-up to find out what was the matter. Dr. Rich, our family doctor, gave me a thorough examination, could find nothing wrong, and then questioned me about my life and work. We discussed my business, the hours that I was working, and my management style. When I finished, he said, "Jim, you can continue what you're doing and make a fortune, but you won't be around long enough to enjoy it. Your problem, plain and simple, is stress. Take my advice, slow down, learn how to delegate, and let go. If you have enough confidence in someone to make him your store manager, then give him the authority and let him do his job. Remember, it's not the amount of time that you put in that makes your business a success. If it was, everyone that worked long hours would be successful, and we both know that's not true. It's the quality of your decisions that will ultimately decide your fate."

I don't recall what that office visit cost, but it was probably the best advice for the money that I have ever gotten.

Manuel Labor

Jim Schindler had just gotten out of the army and was hired at Hagerman's Construction Co., here in Fort Wayne, as a laborer. They were starting to build the Indiana Bank building, with an attached multi-level parking garage. His job consisted of carrying heavy steel reinforcing rods, pushing those two-wheel cement buggies, and other hard physical work. Even though he was still in good shape from the service, by the end of the day, his muscles ached and he was sore all over.

The crew that he worked with was an ethnically diverse group, consisting of about thirty or so men. Approximately a third were Mexican, a third white, and a third black. They were a good bunch of guys and got along well.

Towards the end of an extremely tough day, when he was worn out from carrying large steel rods up the parking ramp to the second and third levels, he went over to a foreman, whose name was

Baker, and said in a serious, hushed voice, "Bake, that Mexican is trying to kill me!"

The foreman glanced worriedly around at the other workers, and then whispered, "Which one…which one?"

"Manuel Labor," Jim replied.

"Schindler, you son of a bitch," he uttered with a grin of relief.

In Plain English

In the United States, a nation made up of people from every country,
culture, and religion in the world, the English language is the
common thread that holds us together.

Why Go?

A friend once asked me, "Why do you go to church every Sunday?"

"Well," I answered, "It's a little bit like working out. When it's over, I always feel better. Besides, I honestly believe that it helps me to be a better person and, heaven knows, I need all the help I can get!"

What a Crack

"Jimmie, did you know that Doss is in Florida?"

"In Florida? You mean I'm up here bustin' mine,
and he's down there layin' on his?"

Hilton's Help

In 1989, my business, Bandido's Restaurante Mexicano, was in a crisis. It was losing two to three hundred thousand dollars a year, and I didn't know how much longer we could hold on. We were looking at every possible way to cut expenses without hurting customer service or quality.

At Bandido's we use cases and cases of lettuce, which we cut up by hand every day. One of our good suppliers suggested that we could save a lot on labor if we bought our lettuce already chopped. He then told us that there was a firm in Cincinnati that would process lettuce to our specifications. We contacted them, and they agreed to put us up at a local hotel if we would drive down to check out their plant and see what a good job, at reasonable prices, they did. If they hadn't paid for our rooms, we would not have gone, because we didn't have the extra money to go.

Within the next few days, Doug Strahm, my Director of Operations, and I drove to Cincinnati. They had made reservations for us at the Hilton Hotel. Little did I know at that time what a profound effect it would have on my life.

We arrived late in the evening, checked in and got ready for bed. After crawling between the sheets, and while shivering until they warmed up, I noticed a paperback book lying on the nightstand. It was the autobiography of Conrad Hilton. I picked it up, thinking about the chain of hotels that he owned, how successful he was, and that maybe there was a lesson in it that could help me. So, I began to read.

It wasn't long before I came to the part about how Mr. Hilton was struggling and was about to lose his entire hotel chain. One day, as he was fighting to save his company and things looked hopeless, he remembered what his mother told him when he was a young boy. "Son," she said, "if ever things go wrong, and you don't know where to turn, say three "Hail Mary's and a prayer to St. Joseph each night, and everything will be okay."

Mr. Hilton had a lot of love and respect for his mother, and I don't know if that was the reason, or because he truly believed that it would help, but he started those prayers. Every night he would get on his knees and say, "Hail Mary, full of grace..." and at the end of each one, he would add a prayer to St. Joseph.

Shortly after he started his prayers, his fortunes began to change, and it wasn't long before his company started to turn around and eventually became one of the world's greatest hotel chains.

Even though I was raised a strict Catholic, I had also pretty much neglected my own faith, but now I was desperate and needed something, anything, to hold on to which would give me the spiritual and mental toughness to get through this crisis. I needed help. That very evening, I started saying three "Hail Mary's and a prayer to St. Joseph. Of course, during this time, we also continued to work as hard and smartly as we could.

Not long after I began my prayers, my situation began to gradually improve, and I soon got the feeling that everything would be okay, just as Mr. Hilton's mother had said it would. I can't prove it, but I know somebody up there answered my prayers, and I believe they'll answer yours if you don't give up!

To this very day, each night at bedtime, I still say my three "Hail Mary's and a prayer to St. Joseph.

You Can't Throw the Bums Out!

The problem with many universities is that they're run

by a bunch of intellectuals, with very little common sense,

that thumb their noses at the world,

while they hide in their ivory towers, protected by tenure.

The Written Word

Unfortunately, some authors write as though their work is a vehicle to display their vast vocabulary, or a showcase for their self-perceived intellectual superiority. Plain and simple, the written word is just a means of communication. If the reader does not understand what is written, then all is for naught.

The Belittled Professor

A couple of years ago I attended a meeting in London at the Portman Hotel with some very successful people. There were six of us in that room, and every one was a multi-millionaire, except my partner, Doss Fisher, and me. One person, an ex-college professor, was doing most of the talking. He went on and on, using words so big that even Daniel Webster would have had to look them up. (Quite frankly, I got the impression that he was just trying to dazzle us with

94

his self-perceived intellectual superiority). I didn't have a clue what he was talking about, but did not want to say anything for fear that everyone else would think that I was about as sharp as a shoulder blade.

Finally, after about fifteen minutes or so, he finished. Following a brief silence, one of the other businessmen said, "What in the hell did he say!"

Nobody knew, but everybody laughed! Then, in an instant, I no longer felt stupid and the professor did. Boy, did I feel better!

The professor never did convince anyone to do the deal, but that night the teacher was taught.

Moral: never give time or money to him who speaks, but cannot be understood.

A Coaching Primer

If it's the coach's job to recruit, to motivate, to teach the fundamentals, to decide the game plan and who plays, then where does the fault lie if the team loses?

The answer is obvious to everyone...except many coaches.

A Warm Wet Feeling

In Bernet Hall at John Carroll University, Fr. Millor was again in rare form. He was grumping at various residents, ordering them around and obviously enjoying his authority, when I said, "Father, you think you're a big wheel, don't you?"

Eyeing me, and not even bothering to take the stogie out of his mouth, he replied, "Yeah!"

"Well, you know what dogs do to wheels!"

The Boss Nose

In April of 1970, Anil Doshi arrived in the United States from India. He was twenty-four, had eight dollars in his pocket and couldn't speak a word of English. His first job was a dishwasher on the graveyard shift, for ten dollars a day...plus food. Through hard work and dedication he moved up through the ranks, and by 1972 he was the general manager of a restaurant in Miami, Florida.

By this time he could speak and understand English pretty well, but was still unfamiliar with many slang expressions and colloquialisms. Each time his boss visited the store, before he left he would tell Anil to keep his nose clean. When he was gone, Anil would rush into the men's room to see if there was anything on or coming out of his nose, but could find nothing. This went on for several months before he finally got the courage to ask his boss. "Why are you always telling me to keep my nose clean? My nose is clean!"

Digital Dialogue

When Anil's boss realized that he didn't understand many American terms or mannerisms, being somewhat of a jokester, he told him that if his car ever broke down and he needed help, all he had to do was to stick out his hand with his middle finger extended, and someone would stop to help him.

As luck would have it, shortly thereafter, Anil's old car conked out. While he stood there, his middle digit pointing skyward, he wondered why the people driving were returning the gesture, with angry looks on their faces. When a silver-haired old lady slowed down, stuck her arm out the window and vigorously gesticulated with her finger, it was obvious to him that she wasn't drying her nails. It was then that he realized something was drastically wrong. So he lowered his middle finger and it joined the others in anonymity.

Soon, a kindly gentleman stopped, gave him a ride and explained the digital dilemma.

To this very day, Anil has never again flipped anyone the bird…well, maybe just once or twice at his old boss!

The Agony of de Seat

I don't know why some women get so upset when a man doesn't lower the toilet seat. I'd think that they'd be happy he raised it.

After all, isn't it easier to put it down than to wipe it off?

Hittin' Bottom

(An Ode to the Porcelain Throne)

"The seat was up again," she said,

As angry as could be.

"I lifted it, to keep it dry,

So you wouldn't get mad," said he.

97

"I sat down," she continued on,

"And fell right in…you lout!"

"My dear," said he, "You might have drowned,

Thank God you bottomed out!"

I wrote the following poem to emphasize the foolishness of the

controversy over which way the toilet tissue should roll,

down the front or back and down along the wall.

Some Tissue Pleeeez!

I had this awful feeling,

When on the porcelain pot.

I reached for a roll to finish the job,

And tissues there were not!

I don't care which way it rolls,

Now that there is none.

It makes no difference up or down,

But please…just get me some!

Fake and Bake

Last Wednesday, my wife Fry and I went to the Village Inn
Restaurant in Roanoke, for dinner. An attractive waitress, with a nice
tan, approached our table and Fry said, "Have you been on vacation?"

"No," she replied, "Why do you ask?"

"You have such a nice tan, I thought that you might have been to Florida."

"It's just a fake and bake. I go to the tanning salon."

"Don't worry," I kidded, "I think you look tanfastic!"

A Reason to Rise

If you don't have a reason to get up in the
morning, it won't be long and you won't!

Paraphrasing Parker

Men seldom make passes,
At girls with big asses!

Parts are Falling

It has been a little over a year ago since Dr. Buchholtz operated on my fourteen-year-old daughter Rachel's back. On Monday, she injured her hip while running track.

"Rachel," my wife said, "Dave Kuhn (the physical therapist) said that you should have it X-rayed."

"Which doctor am I going to?" Rachel wanted to know.

"Dr. Buchholtz."

"Dr. Buchholtz!" exclaimed Rachel. "He's going to think I'm falling apart!"

The Quiet Woman

Charlie's mother died, and true to her wishes, he had her cremated. It was a beautiful Indiana summer day when he got a call from the mortuary that his mother's ashes were ready to be picked up. So he stopped, claimed the urn with her remains and headed to the lake to spend the day.

About halfway there, he looked over at his mother sitting on the front seat and said, "Mom, this is the first time that you ever rode to the lake with me without bitchin' about my driving!"

Oh...Sick!

What the hell is this?" Charlie thought as he examined a small pouch of foil that had just found in his freezer. It contained a grayish sticky substance. He put his finger in it, touched it to his tongue, and said to himself, "This crap is awful!"

That evening, when his roommate, John, came home, Charlie asked, "What's this stuff?" as he showed him the foiled bag.

John's eyes lit up. "I've been looking for that. It's heroin."

He then heated some on the stove and added a few drops of some sort of a colorless fluid. When the whole concoction liquefied and turned clear, he sucked some up into a syringe, tied off his arm to make the veins pop out, waited until it cooled and injected himself.

In no time at all, he turned various shades of green, threw up all over himself and fell down on the floor. As Charlie watched him lying there, quivering and shaking as though suffering from a convulsion, he thought, "The son of a bitch is going to die on me!" In what seemed like forever, but was probably only a few minutes, John pulled himself up, sat down at the kitchen table and said, as he slid the syringe over to Charlie, "Wow, man, that was great…Wanna try some?"

I'm Holding Me Down

Most people can't rise above themselves!

They are prisoners of their minds, captives of their thinking.

For spring break I took the family to Siesta Key in Florida.

After spending some time on the beach,

I wrote the following poems, based on my observations.

Naturally

She wore a bikini so small

to the beach, as he watched her in awe.

For he hoped she'd jump in to the sea for a swim

And come out…au natural!

He Looked, But Did Not See!

She lay on the beach with a book,

In a bikini that caught every look.

As he strolled slowly by, with just her in his eye,

A stumble and tumble he took!

The Devil's Own

Joe lives in the country, on a farm, outside of Monroe, Indiana. He owns a woodworking shop, and does beautiful work. However, being Amish, he doesn't believe in modern conveniences such as electricity, automobiles, telephones, etc. Instead, the Amish still use horse and buggies, kerosene lamps, and live like they did in the eighteen hundreds. Hence, whenever Joe needs to get in touch with a supplier or customer, he has his driver (obviously not of the same persuasion) take him down the road a few miles in his van to the nearest phone.

"Joe, wouldn't it be a lot easier if you installed a telephone?" I asked.

"Oh, I couldn't do that," he answered. "It's against our ways."

Sometime later, I told my son John about this conversation, and he remarked, "I guess that means it's okay to use the devil...you just can't own him."

Joe Knows

"Did you hear that Joe just had his fifteenth kid?"

"He did?"

"Yeah."

"Well, I'd tell him where to put it, but I guess he already knows."

A Funny Quaaack

"Can you tell a duck from a goose?"

"Heck, yes. I know a goose when I feel one!"

Something to Ponder

In nature, "Natural Selection," also known as the survival of the fittest, is the universal law. It ensures the continuation of a species by seeing that only the genes of the most intelligent and strongest are passed on, since the weak and sick (mentally and physically), either die prematurely or cannot compete with the fittest in the reproduction process.

Today, however, with regard to the "Human Race," nature's law doesn't seem to apply. Science and modern medicine have saved many of the sick and feeble that would surely have died naturally only a few decades ago, and I wouldn't change that or have it any other way.

Still, I wonder, since nature's (natural selection's) role is greatly diminished, are we passing on more and more undesirable traits that will sooner or later seriously weaken our species? Moreover, is the continuation of scientific research and progress paramount, since it may be the only hope for the survival of a species weakened by the absence of the natural selection process?

Eli's

Eli ran a strip joint that he named in his honor. The girls would dance provocatively on top of the bar and disrobe seductively in front of the panting customers. One night, he brought his ninety-two-year-old father to the club. They sat at the bar, and unbeknownst to his dad, he told his sexiest stripper to put on a show for him. She danced, shimmied, squirmed, and took it all off. When she was completely in the buff, she bent over and wiggled her derriere just a foot or so in front of his face.

The old guy looked at her behind, then at his son, and said, "What am I supposed to do…wipe it?"

People Power

Technology be damned! The most important factor
in any company's success is still its people.

Moron TV

A TV camera is the only device I know that can instantly turn
reasonably normal people into grinning, screaming, gesticulating
idiots!

Hate

It is extremely hard to make good decisions if you are full of
hate and prejudice, for they cloud the mind and distort reality.

No Invitation

I once had a restaurant in Portland, Indiana, called Jimmie's Pizza. As I was going through its monthly financial statements, I noticed that the cost of liquor was extremely high. This indicated that either someone was stealing or giving away a lot of drinks.

I called in Randy Brubaker, who did some consulting and troubleshooting for me. "Randy," I said, "We've got a problem with our liquor cost in Portland. I want you to run down there and find out what's going on."

Randy drove to Portland and hung out in the bar, getting to know the bartenders and staff. (They had no idea who he was). In a few days, he dropped by my office and told me that he had figured out what the problem was.

"What is it?" I wanted to know.

"After the assistant manager closes at night, he comes back an hour or so later with some of his friends and has a party, and you're paying for their drinks."

"Are you sure?"

"Hell, yes," he answered, "They asked me to join them. You put on a great party, boss," he said, rubbing it in.

"Do you know what really pisses me off?" I said, quite irritated.

"What?"

"I paid for their damn party, and they didn't even have the decency to invite me!"

You Don't Say!
Sometimes, what people don't say
says more than what they say!

The Real Root

Money is not the root of all evil…it's greed.

Greed is what makes people do

all kinds of evil things to acquire money.

Want Worms?

The early bird gets the worm.

But who wants worms?

Real Worth

A person's real worth is in his character, not his pocketbook!

Where's Mr. Honda When You Need Him?

How come they can make cars that can go 100,000 miles

without a problem, but they can't make a boat that will go

one summer (three months) without many?

Picture Perfect

You can buy a picture postcard of almost any famous site in the world

that would probably be a lot more professional than your snapshot of

it.

But if you truly want to take a memorable photo of something well

known, make sure a family member, friend, or you are in the picture.

Oral Denial

If oral sex isn't sex, why do they call it that?
And isn't denying that it is just a way for Slick Willie
and others to have sex without admitting that they did?

Do It...Your Way!

If everyone's doing it, it's wrong.
Not because it's incorrect, but because everyone's doing it!

Faceless

If you're just another face in the crowd, you're faceless!

Feeling Natural

Today, we are led by many social workers, therapists, psychologists, psychiatrists, and other do-gooder busy bodies, to believe that if we show any negative emotions such as anger, despair, disappointment or sadness, we need counseling or therapy. Excuse me...but aren't these emotions as natural as the emotions of love and joy? And could it be that they are just part of being human? If so, why should we feel guilty, ashamed, or made to believe that we need counseling because we have natural human emotions?

A Miraculous Cure

I once had a manager whose teenage son became so mad when his dad wouldn't let him do whatever he wanted that he ran away. That evening a police officer saw him wandering the streets, picked him up and returned him home. His father, being quite concerned, took him to a well-advertised counseling center. The counselor asked several questions, and after determining that he was covered by insurance, decided his son needed therapy.

The counseling went on for several months, and by some strange coincidence, the same time the insurance ran out, miracle of miracles, the boy was cured! Which makes me wonder who benefited the most, the counseling center's bank account, or the boy?

A Heavenly Halloween

Every Halloween, the staff at Bandido's Mexican Restaurant wears costumes (limited only by their imagination), to the delight of the guests. On this particular festival of the dead, two Catholic priests, Father Jeff and Father Jim, came in for dinner and, lo and behold... guess who waited on them? A waitress dressed as a pregnant nun! As she walked up to greet them, she said, "Nice costumes, guys," and then took their drink order.

At the bar, when she was informed that the two gentlemen were actually priests, being Halloween, she was extremely *horrified.* Returning to their table, she kept her eyes lowered in shame as she set down their drinks and muttered, "Bless me, Father, for I have sinned."

To which Father Jeff answered, "You are forgiven, my child. Now for your penance, you may pay for our dinner," which she did, making that hollow evening... heavenly, for the clever clerics!

Goodbye, Bobby

Wimpy heard that his old friend Bobby was going to have surgery, so he stopped by Lambro's, Bobby's restaurant, to see him. "What ya got?" Wimpy asked.

"I've got an aneurysm," Bobby replied.

"What's that?"

"It's a bulge, like a balloon, in my blood vessel, that could break and cause a stroke or I could bleed to death."

Wimpy leaned back in the booth, pulled away from Bobby, raised his hand fingers extended, and then rapidly waved goodbye.

A few weeks later, Bobby was home recuperating from his operation, when Wimpy dropped by to see him. "Why didn't you come up to the hospital and visit me?" Bobby asked, somewhat disappointed.

"I did," Wimpy exclaimed, "but you looked half dead, so I left!"

Not to Worry

My fourteen-year-old son Jimmie and I were driving down the road when I wanted to use the car phone. "Damn, I can't remember Doss' phone number," I said in sheer frustration.

Jimmie then rattled off the number.

"How'd you know his number?" I asked.

"Dad, I'm not old, I have a good memory!" He then reached over, patted me on the leg and continued, "But don't worry, Dad, we won't put you in a nursing home."

Ears to You

Around the same time, Jimmie said something to me and I asked, "What did you say?" He then repeated himself and I said, somewhat annoyed, "Talk louder, I can't hear you."

Raising his voice, he blurted out, "Dad…1-800-Miracle Ear."

I Can't Get There

I hate it when I don't know where I'm going,

because when I don't know where I'm going,

I never get there!

Clean Enough

My daughter Rachel totaled her car, and a good friend of ours, Tom Hire, of Hire's Auto Parts, lent her an old car to use until we could replace it. After a week or two, we found a great, low mileage, used Alero that she liked, and bought it. The day we brought the new (new to Rachel, that is) car home, I told Rachel to clean up Mr. Hire's car and we would take it back to him.

That evening, when I returned home, stuck on the outside of the kitchen door was a "Post It" note with the following message: "Dad, Mr. Hire's car is as clean as it's gonna get! Rachie."

Next

Rachel is also a junior at Bishop Luers High School, and for one reason or another has decided to transfer after the first semester to Bishop Dwenger High School, also here in Fort Wayne.

Last week in religion class, all the students were asked to take turns in saying a short prayer. When it was her turn, one girl, who didn't particularly care for Rachel, got up and sarcastically said, "Let's pray for all the students that are transferring to Bishop Dwenger." (Rachel was the only one).

Rachel immediately jumped up and said, "I don't need your prayers! Next!"

Sorry Ben

Remember the old adage, "A poor excuse is better than none"? Quite frankly, I believe that it rings truer to say, "A poor excuse is worse than none."

Dumb Teaching

A while ago, when my sister first heard that they were going to teach Ebonics in the classroom, she was so surprised and taken aback that she blurted out, "You mean they're going to teach them to talk stupid?"

The Fool

A fool is one who knows not,
And knows not that he knows not,

But thinks he knows.

S...M...I...T...H

At a party, my brother-in-law Hank Freistroffer was introduced to a gentleman with whom he talked for quite awhile. About three months later, rather unexpectedly, he ran into him again.

The gentleman greeted him with a firm handshake and said, "Hi, Hank, how are you doing?"

"Fine," Hank replied, with a furrowed brow, trying to remember his name.

After some more small talk, Hank had a brilliant idea. I'll just ask him how he spells his name, and that way I'll find out what it is.

So as soon as he had the opportunity to work it into the conversation, he asked, "How do you spell your last name?"

The gentleman looked curiously at Hank and then spelled it very slowly, clearly enunciating each letter, "S...M...I...T...H."

Promise!

If Jesus, Buddha, Muhammad and all of the religious leaders throughout the ages could not please everyone, how can we expect to? No matter what you do, someone will be "agin" it. Consequently, if you just do your best, ignore the naysayers and get on with your life, you'll find that everything will turn out all right... promise!

Experience

Experience is always valued a lot more by those who have it!

Sammy Called

After Jimmy D'Angelo's bypass operation, his brother Sam called a close friend of theirs, Bill Eshcoff, to let him know how well the operation had gone. After he explained how great Jimmy was doing, Bill said, "You tell him that he cost me five dollars."

"How's that?" Sam asked.

"Because I bet my brother Bobby five bucks that he wouldn't make it!"

You Tell Them

Our Bandido's Mexican Restaurant, located on Winchester Road, just outside of Ft. Wayne, Indiana, does very well. On one extremely busy Friday night, the parking lot was full, so our guests began parking along the road, with two wheels on the pavement and two on the berm. By now, the lobby was packed with customers waiting to be seated and things were somewhat hectic, when in walked a deputy sheriff.

"Are you the manager?" he asked.

"I'm not the manager, but I'm the owner," I answered.

"I want you to tell everyone who's parked along the road to move their cars."

"Wait a minute," I said. "That's not my job; you're the cop - you tell them!"

Confused by the facts, and not knowing what to do next, he looked down at the floor, shook his head in disbelief and then walked out the door, gone but not forgotten!

Backpat

Don't pat yourself too hard on the back.

It will not only irritate others,

but you might break your damn arm!

Grooming and Grammar

It is wise to remember that

all first impressions are based on two things:

appearance and speech!

Picky...Picky

One good thing about picky people,

they have clean noses!

Their Egos Again!

Many times, on TV and in the other media, movie stars and various other popular entertainers are quoted and believed as though they were experts on a wide range of subjects that have nothing to do with their profession. However, I for one, have never put much credence in their comments, because how does someone's ability to mouth another's words qualify them as an expert on anything?

Bad is Good!

Yesterday, Mel Gibson, the movie star, and an exception to the previous comments, was being interviewed on TV and he said something that I believe rings true. He said, "Even a bad experience is good, if you learn something from it!"

Pretty Ugly

At one of our Bandido's Restaurants, we have a lady bartender who is as good with the guests as she is at bartending. Even though she is well-groomed, she is, as one might say to be charitable, homely. Others, being less refined, would probably say that she is downright ugly.

On entering Bandidos, our Vice President, Anil Doshi, was accosted by an irate customer sitting at the bar. "I'm mad at you," he said as he grabbed Anil's arm to stop him, so he'd listen.

"Why are you mad at me?" Anil wanted to know.

"Because your bartender shut me off last night. She said that I had too much to drink!"

"Did you tell her she was beautiful?" Anil asked.

"Yeah."

"Then you must have been drunk!"

Oink Oink

The trouble with eating like a pig
is that sooner or later, you'll look like one!

Crazy Drivers

If there are no idiots,

what do you call all of the crazy drivers?

He Has Ears, But Does Not Want To Hear!

During a routine check-up, Bobby Eshcoff's doctor found an aneurysm near his heart and recommended an operation to correct the problem. On the scheduled day, as Bobby lay on the cart, waiting to be wheeled into surgery, his daughter Nancy, an attorney, stood there with a yellow legal pad cradled in her arm and began to question the surgeon as Bobby listened.

"What are the chances of a stroke?" she asked him.

"About one in twenty," the doctor answered.

"What about paralysis?"

"About the same, one in twenty, but we don't really worry about that..."

"What do you worry about?" Nancy interjected

"About death."

"Death!" she repeated, surprised and somewhat taken aback.

"Put that god-damned pad away," Bobby groaned, not wanting to hear anymore.

Short Changed

In the 1970s, a group of guys, who loved to argue and get on each other's cases, hung out at Lambro's bar. On this particular evening, after a few libations, Mike Holly and Paul Hook were going at it when the discussion became quite heated. Finally, in sheer frustration, Mike looked at Paul, and exclaimed, "What the hell do you know; you don't even wear shorts!"

"The hell I don't!" Paul answered, raising his voice.

"Bet you twenty bucks you don't!"

"Okay, but just a minute, I have to go to the john," Paul informed Mike.

As Paul stood there taking care of business, Jimmy D'Angelo, one of the guys, walked into the restroom. Like a bolt from the netherworld, a "gutter-al" idea struck Paul. After explaining his bet with Mike, he asked and Jimmy agreed to give him his shorts.

Meanwhile, just entering Lambro's was Harold Toepfer, another regular, felt the urge and entered the men's room. On seeing Paul and Jimmy standing there trouserless, and Jimmy handing Paul his shorts, Harold made a hasty exit.

Returning to the table, and listening to more accusations about his lack of underwear, Paul unloosened his belt, and dropped his trousers, displaying his newfound white boxers.

"Those aren't yours...you bastard, you never wear underpants!" Mike yelled, becoming irritated at the thought of the razzing he'd have to take from the guys, for losing the bet to Paul.

"Well, who in the hell's shorts do you think I got on, you cheap ass? Now pay up!" Mike did, and to this very day, he is still none the wiser that he was short-changed!

Finger Pointing

When Bobby Eschoff was young, he used to bartend for Wimpy Rodenbeck, whom he called Boss. After mixing a few drinks one evening, he noticed Wimpy walk into the bar, and greeted him with, "Hi, Boss, how's your sex life?"

Not saying a word, Wimpy raised his right hand, like he was taking an oath, and then quickly bent his wrist so that all fingers were pointing at the floor. Bobby laughed…Wimp was limp!

No Lie

Last night, at Bishop Luers High School's annual fundraiser, John (Mac) McCormick, a mortician, was seated at Bishop D'Arcy's table. When the bishop came over to take his seat, he noticed a single red rose on his place setting for him to pin onto his lapel. As he tried to attach it to his coat, Mac said, "Bishop, I'd pin that on for you, but you'd have to lie down!"

Now That Smarts!

A couple of months ago, my wife Fry told Bobby Eschcoff and his wife Natka about the fairy tale that I had written for my daughter, Heidi. After Fry's glowing review, they asked if they could read it, so I gave them a copy.

Several weeks later, we saw Bobby at his restaurant (Lambros) and he came over and sat down with us.

"I read your story," he said, "and it was very good. The way you described things almost made me feel like I was there. Natka read it to all the grandchildren. But," he went on, "I was really surprised that **you** wrote it."

"Why was that?" I foolishly asked.

"Because I didn't think you were that smart!"

He's So Proud

Back in the 1970s, I was watching, along with my brother, Joe, the TV show "All in the Family," featuring that famous bigot, Archie Bunker. After one of Archie's usual tirades, I asked Joe, who was also very opinionated, if Archie reminded him of anyone he knew. "Yeah," he replied, "and I'm damn proud of it!"

The Agony of de Seat (belt)

In Indiana, we have a mandatory seat belt law and if you get caught without one, it's a twenty-five dollar fine. Recently, my friend Henry Husmann was pulled over for not wearing his, and he explained to the state trooper that he'd had a pacemaker installed about a month ago and the shoulder strap hurt him when he wore it.

"That's funny," the officer said as he handed him a ticket, "My father also had one put in a few weeks ago, and he wears his!"

Pudd'n and Why?

An old saying goes, "The proof is in the pudding."

Perhaps better put would be, "The proof is in the performance."

It Was Really Big!

Before "MADD Mothers" and all the uproar over drinking and driving, I must confess that one evening I'd had more than I should have; or, to quote an old saying, "I had a snoot full." On the drive home, Broadway (Street) was lightly covered with gently falling snow, and as I drove through the railroad underpass near the GE, I kicked it because the pavement under it was dry. As soon as I came out of the underpass and was again on the snow-covered pavement, my car did a one-eighty, slid backwards down the street and slammed into a huge General Electric plant.

The police were called and Officer George Pappas pulled up, took one look at the situation and said, "How in the heck could anyone hit the GE?"

"It was so damn big," I said, slurring my words, "I couldn't miss it!"

Ian

For many years, Ian Rolland was president of the Lincoln Life Insurance Company, based here in Fort Wayne, one of the largest insurance companies in the United States. He was, and still is, well-respected, not only locally, but also throughout the entire insurance industry.

He is a graduate of DePauw University, in Greencastle, Indiana, and is one of their more prominent alumni. Since his retirement, I run into him occasionally at the local YMCA. One day, I saw him there and informed him that DePauw was recruiting Jimmie and Heidi, my son and daughter, and that I told them that they didn't want to go there.

"Why not?" he asked with a look of disappointment.

Because I told them that, "Ian Rolland went there and you don't want to turn out like him!"

Ian forced a smile.

No Yeast

Last Friday, Jim Schindler had a toothache and called his dentist, Dr. Friedrick. "I'm sorry, Dr. Fredrick is off this afternoon," he was told by the receptionist. "But if you can come in at about two o'clock, Dr. Kim Druley can see you."

At the appointed time, she examined him, looked at the X-rays that Amber, her technician had just taken, and told him that his tooth was infected.

"I'll prescribe an antibiotic that will help clear up the infection," she explained, "And you can make an appointment with Dr. Friedrick next week."

"An antibiotic?" he asked.

"Yes," she responded.

"It won't give me a yeast infection, will it?"

Dr. Druley and Amber both roared. It was the yeast they could do!

The Best Compliment Ever

A few months ago, as my nineteen-year-old son, Jimmie, and I were driving home from the movies, he asked me if I knew who his best friend was.

"George Leugers," I guessed.

"No."

"Dan Bowers?"

"No.

"Zack?"

"Nope."

"I give up, who?"

"You are, Dad!"

He Knows One

Someone's name came up in a conversation with a friend of mine.

"He's an asshole," my friend commented.

"Do you know him?" I asked.

"No-o-o-o," was his reply.

"Well, I guess you know one, even if you don't know one!"

Legal Extortion

Not too many years ago, some lawyers would go to hospitals and encourage accident victims to sue whomever was in the general area. As a result, they were called ambulance chasers. We still have lawyers who do the same thing today; the only difference is that they advertise their services on TV. One might call them "Electronic Ambulance Chasers." Even if they don't believe that there is a legal basis for a suit, and they know that their clients don't have a ghost of a chance in court, they still take the case, knowing full well that many businesses and insurance companies will settle out of court because it is cheaper than litigating the case. If the insurance company decides to fight, many of these suits are quickly dropped.

This practice is not only limited to personal injury cases but is also widely used in other situations, such as job terminations, even if they were justified. By telling the client that there will be no fee unless they receive compensation, the greedy client has nothing to lose and agrees to the legal action. In the time it takes to write a simple letter threatening a lawsuit, the lawyer is almost certain that there will be some sort of a settlement offer, and, of course, a nice fee for him or her, since it would be much cheaper for the companies to settle than to fight it. If this is not legal extortion, I don't know what else any rational person would call it!

The only way to stop this legal extortionary practice is to pass a law that if you sue someone and lose, you must pay their attorney fees and other reasonable costs. (Better yet, make their attorneys split those costs). Then, and only then, will this plethora of frivolous lawsuits end and the logjam that now burdens our courts be broken.

Justly Deserved

Do you know how lawyers got such a bad reputation?

They got it the old-fashioned way…they earned it!

Good God, Gayle!

Tilly was chatting with her old friend, sixty-five-year-old Gayle Ainsworth, as they were sitting at the bar in the Eagles Lodge. While they were bantering back and forth, to emphasize a point, she put his hand on Gayle's leg.

"Good God, Gayle!" she said, somewhat surprised. "You sure got a skinny leg!"

"Why, that isn't my leg!" Gayle grinned, as he took another swig of beer!

Economics 102

Miz Lehman, a successful realtor and businessman in Berne, a small Indiana town surrounded by a fairly good-sized Amish farm community, told me this story, which he claims really happened.

Back in the 1970s, a local businessman went to the town bank to ask for a $100,000 loan and was turned down. A few weeks later, he learned of an Amish farmer who had applied for a loan of the same size and got it. In a fit of rage the businessman marched over to his hometown bank and angrily asked, "Why did you turn me down? I make a hell of a lot more money than that Amish man!"

"That may be true," answered the loan officer, "but how much do you keep?"

One Ding—A—Ling

I am an usher at St. Peter's Catholic Church. Built in 1893, it is a well-maintained, beautiful old Gothic edifice. Every Sunday, five minutes before mass starts, one of the ushers must ring the steeple bells, by standing in the entranceway and pulling a long, thick rope, which goes clear up to the bell tower. The bells are large and, when I get them swinging, I always have had this irresistible urge to hang onto the rope to see if it will pull me up.

One Sunday, as I was ringing them, no one was in the foyer and I thought that now would be a perfect time to see if the swinging bells had enough weight and momentum to lift me off the floor. So I hung on and as soon as I did, a family of four walked into the church and looked with astonishment at this sixty-five-year-old, gray-haired-man, hanging onto the rope with his feet off the ground. As soon as my feet were back on terra firma, I shrugged my shoulders and said, "Some people will do anything for a free ride!"

Hot or Cool?

Sometimes I hear my teenage daughter Rachel, when she sees a good-looking boy, say, "He's hot!" And sometimes she says, "He's cool!" Which makes me wonder why, when I'm hot, I'm not cool?

The Naked Truth

A year or so ago, a national magazine, inserted in many Sunday newspapers, sponsored a poetry contest. The top prize was awarded to a young high school student and his poem was printed for all to see. After reading it, I had no idea what it was about or what it meant, so I asked my son, Jimmie, and daughter, Heidi, both national honor students, to read it so that they could explain it to me. Neither one had the foggiest idea what it meant. Even the magazine's columnist, in his interview with the young man, had to ask him to explain what this or that was all about.

Personally, I think that this is a classic example of "The King's New Clothes," an old fairy tale about a king who was conned by two slippery tailors into believing that anyone not fit for his office, couldn't see the beautiful clothes they had made for him. Of course, the king pretended to see the clothing, while the tailors explained how beautiful and rich the material was, as they dressed him in preparation for a festival and parade. As the king walked through the city, everyone, for obvious reasons, pretended to see the beautiful attire, until a little boy yelled, "Look, the King is naked!"

In reference to the poetry competition, I believe that one or more of the judges exclaimed how wonderful and profound the poem was and the rest of the judges, not understanding it, or worse, not wanting to appear ignorant, agreed… and it won first prize! Oh well, at least Keats, Byron, and Shelley won't have to worry.

Finally, could it be that if one cannot understand what is written, the modern day consensual thinking is that the work has to be an intellectual masterpiece and the author a genius? Perhaps if it were understood, the naked truth would be exposed!

Entitled

We all know folks who have a very high opinion
of their opinion. Nevertheless, I'd like to
point out that everyone is entitled to his opinion
…no matter how erroneous!

Not Too Cool!

Many times, during the freezing winter months here in
Indiana, I have heard a lot of my friends say, "I hate this cold
weather!" I then explain that I like our four seasons, and that includes
wintertime. After that, I go on to say, "In the winter, I can always put
on enough clothes to keep warm, but on a hot day I can't always take
enough off to keep cool… without looking ridiculous!"

I Got Ya Covered!

"Better safe than sorry,"
sayeth the prophylactic salesman.

A Judicial System Run Amok

Many money-grubbing media lawyers and their greedy, sue-
happy clients that they pursued are being awarded huge sums of
money in frivolous lawsuits that should have been thrown out of
court, by any rational judge.

A case in point: how could anyone be awarded millions of
dollars for spilling hot coffee on herself is beyond my, or any other
reasonable person's, comprehension! Common sense tells us that if

she were served cold coffee, she would angrily return it and demand her money back. The judge who allowed this case to go to trial was truly suffering from "uppis," (his head was uppis his derrière). I can't even imagine where the jury's heads were!

Quite recently, some sleazy lawyer dug up a client willing to sue a particular restaurant chain, because he supposedly got fat eating there. Excuse me, but unless they tied him down and rammed food down his throat, this ridiculous case should have been immediately thrown out of court. If not, this action only reinforces the growing consensus that no matter what we do, someone else is responsible and no one is to be held accountable, for his or her actions. Again, any reasonable judge should have given this case, along with the sleazy lawyer and his gluttonous client, the heave-ho...unless, of course, he is suffering from "uppis."

Let A Sleeping Student Lie

My son Jimmie has really been hitting the books at John Carroll University, because he applied to transfer to the University of Notre Dame and knows that he will need very good grades. He expects a letter of rejection or admission from them, within a few days.

After his final exams, very little sleep and a four-hour drive, he finally arrived home from college, exhausted. He then announced that he was going to bed and that there were only four reasons that he wanted to be awakened: if the Pope called; if he received a letter from

Notre Dame; if a supermodel wanted him; or if Publisher's Clearing House knocked on his door. We let him sleep!

Airs

Some people like to "put on airs." Quite frankly, I believe they'd feel a lot better if they'd just expel some!

Elvis, Who?

It was either in 1955, or 1956, while I was attending John Carroll University in Cleveland, Ohio, when one of my buddies, Dave Bresnahan, asked me if I wanted to go to a concert with him.

"I don't know," I replied. "Who's playing?"

"Elvis Presley," he answered.

"Who's he? I never heard of him."

"You'll like him. He's kind of a cross between country and rock and roll."

Not having anything better to do, I went. I'd never seen anything like it! It was electrifying! It was as though someone had put a finger into an electrical socket and everyone held hands. It was really dynamic! As we were leaving the theatre, I again asked Dave, "What did you say his name was?"

"Elvis Presley."

"Elvis Presley," I repeated. "That's a funny name; he ought to change it. Nobody's gonna remember that!"

Pinchie...Pinchie!

In 1968, I opened my first restaurant, "Jimmie's Pizza Inn." Saturday afternoons were pretty slow, so in addition to making the pizza, I also waited on tables. On this particular Saturday, three girls in their mid-twenties came in. When I'd finished taking their order and was about to go make their pizza, one of the girls jokingly (I think) said, "What would you do if I pinched your butt?"

"Why, I'd turn around real quick!"

They all laughed, but no pinchie...pinchie. Shucks!

Never-ending

Love is a wonderful thing:

the more you give, the more you get.

And no matter how much love you give,

you never run out!

Nice Guys Finish First

It is very unfortunate that many folks believe the old expression "Nice guys finish last." However, that is as far from the truth as one could possibly get. The vast majority of the most successful people, be it in business or any other profession, are probably the nicest people that you could possibly meet.

John Donne once said, "No man is an island," which is precisely why nice guys finish first. No matter what we do, we must work with and deal with others. Anyone who is foolish enough to be unfair, dishonest, inconsiderate or disrespectful to his or her co-workers, employees, or customers, will eventually lose their good will and cooperation, making it impossible to succeed in any profession or enterprise.

To move up the ladder, in any endeavor, requires the help and support of many people. Only if you earn their respect and cooperation will they assist you in reaching the top. This is exactly why the higher up you go in any organization, the nicer the people. Of course, there are exceptions (there are exceptions to every rule), but overall, the basic principles necessary to succeed dictate that, "Nice guys really do finish first!"

Knock...Knock

Stan was particularly fond of the grape. As a matter of fact, he was fond of anything fermented or distilled. One evening, after over-indulging in his favorite beverage, he headed home. It was about a twenty-mile trip down a two-lane country highway and he was having trouble, as one is apt to have when inebriated, focusing on his driving and the road.

To complicate his problem, Stan found himself driving in a heavy snowstorm, straining to see the road, as his wipers struggled to keep up with the snow that peppered his windshield. Suddenly, he heard someone knock on his car window. He looked at the speedometer. He was doing forty-five mph. Again, rap...rap...rap, on the snow-covered driver's side window. Afraid, and trying to shake the fog from his alcohol-soaked brain, with a great deal of anxiety,

Stan slowly lowered the window, wondering how anyone could be knocking on his window at 45 mph.

As soon as the window was open enough to peek out, a Good Samaritan standing there said, "Hey, buddy, do you need a ride?"

As the mist that clouded his mind slowly dissipated, Stan soon realized that he was sitting in a cornfield, stuck in the snow and mud, spinning his tires and doing 45 mph.

After he told this story, I wiped the tears of laughter from my eyes and asked him what he thought when he heard someone banging on his window.

"It scared the hell out of me so bad," he answered, "that I thought I was going to have an accident!"

More is Better!

Many people watch their spending very carefully, trying their best to make ends meet and keep the wolf from the door. However, if they'd concentrated on how to make more money, instead of on how to pinch pennies, they'd probably never again have to worry about the "big bad wolf."

Wheels Are Turning

My son, Jimmie, and my daughter, Heidi, stopped at Taco Bell for lunch. Getting out of the car, Jimmie said, "Heidi, look how far the handicapped parking spots are from the front door."

"What difference does it make?" Heidi replied. "They've got wheels!"

Reilly's Brackets

I'm sure that almost everyone is aware that on all profit and loss statements, when the bottom line has parentheses around the number, it indicates that the business lost money for that period or month.

Reilly only had a third grade education, but was a very successful businessman, who owned approximately forty various franchised restaurants. He sold burgers, pizza, chicken, and seafood, and did it very well. One day Jim, a friend of mine, was in Reilly's office and questioned him, "Reilly, how in the hell did you do it? Most men with college degrees haven't done as well as you. How'd ya do it?"

"Aw," Reilly replied in his best good-ol'-boy accent, "It ain't so hard. When I get the monthly financial statements from each store, I just look at the bottom line, and if it has brackets around it, I fire the son-of-a-bitch!"

A Sad Commentary

A lot of people die when they either have nothing to live for, or when life becomes too painful.

A Dressing Down

Jimmie was home on college break, when he volunteered at St. Patrick's Clothing Bank, to help hand out items to the poor and disadvantaged. He showed up looking like a typical college kid, wearing some old grungy clothes and a stocking hat. After working several hours, and just as he was about to leave, Father Largent approached him with this clever observation: "Jimmie," he said, "Even though you've been working with the underprivileged, I didn't expect you to look like one!"

Accidentally

In spite of all the well-meaning, frivolous legislation, and the good intentions of our lawmakers, they will never succeed in making our land accident-free. Accidents will always happen. By its very definition, an accident is something that happens by chance or an unknown cause. That's why they call them accidents. Probably, the only way that you can be perfectly safe is to stay in bed all day. Then if the roof doesn't fall in on you, the damn place will probably burn down! By accident, of course!

Now That's Zit-tifull

Did you know that you're never too old to get a zit?

A Politician's Priority

A politician's number one (#1) priority is to get re-elected, and most of them will say, do, or promise almost anything (whether it is or isn't in the best interest of their constituents or the country), that will get them the most votes. Wouldn't it make more sense if we limited all politicians to one term? Then perhaps they could focus more on their responsibilities to the taxpayers and vote for what is truly best for the country and their constituents, instead of worrying and scheming on how to get re-elected?

For example, the President and Congress would be limited to one six-year term. The terms for the Senate and House would be staggered, so that one third of the seats would be up for election every two years. (This staggered system would ensure continuity.) States, counties, cities, etc., would then follow the same formula.

However, this method makes so much sense that I can almost guarantee you that most politicians wouldn't support it, since it would most certainly prevent them from endlessly sucking on the taxpayer's tits!

Something's Fishy

Give a man a fish, and you feed him for a day,

show him how to fish, and he'll miss a lot of work.

Some Sobering Lessons

Jack Daniels, Mr. Gallo, and his good friend, Mr. Budweiser, have taught me, too many times the hard way, the following lessons:

- After a few drinks, you can't do anything as well as you could before. This includes thinking, working, playing, and the pursuit of amour. Booze just makes you think you can! A wise man once said, "Alcohol increaseth the desire, but ruineth the performance!"

- With each drink, you lose a little more control over your brain, your motor skills, and worst of all…your tongue!
- You can't reason with liquor.
- The next day, you and the quality of your performance will suffer in direct proportion to the severity of your hangover.

Experience the Experience

With each new experience, one gains knowledge, skill, and confidence.

And also with that newly-acquired experience…a greater understanding.

The Devil You Say

The difference between the Mideastern fanatics

and us is that if they do something bad, they do it in the name of God.

If we do something bad, the devil made us do it!

It Must Be That Time!

There is a bathroom adjoining my wife's and my bedroom. There is also an entrance to this bathroom from the hallway. Yesterday, as I was looking for something in my bedroom closet, Rachel, our eighteen-year-old daughter, opened the bathroom door to our bedroom and all that I could see was her head sticking through. "Dad," she informed me, with a big grin on her face as her hand appeared through the door, shaking a tampon, "Don't come in here for a couple of minutes."

No Titillating Tell

Joe was taking his ninety-one-year-old dad, Bill, (who suffered somewhat of a short-term memory loss), home, when his dad wanted to stop for a beer. They pulled into a local tavern, had a couple of beers, and then continued on their way home. "Son," Bill inquired, "What is that place?" pointing at what looked like another bar.

"Dad, that's Cagney's, a strip joint,"

"Let's stop and get a beer,"

"Okay," Joe answered, "but don't tell mom or the girls...they'll kill me."

"Don't worry," Dad pointed out, "By the time I get home, I'll have forgotten all about it!"

Guiltless

If your grandfather whipped mine, would you be guilty of assault? If not, then why should you be held responsible for any wrongdoing that occurred generations ago?

What Happened?

Unfortunately, in these times, too many people believe that they can get rich by either ripping someone off, or by suing them, which, in many cases, is the same thing. Whatever happened to the old-fashioned belief that if you want to get ahead, you have to work hard and get a good education?

Quite a Feet

Did you ever notice that no matter how tall or short
a person is, their feet always reach the ground?

Why Ask?

Even tho' we men refuse to ask for directions,
none of us have ever been lost permanently...yet!

A Legal Dilemma

At the risk of MADD-ening the Mothers, I'd like to point out that young people of eighteen, nineteen, or twenty years of age are legally adults. Why then, shouldn't they be able to drink alcoholic beverages and enjoy the same rights as the rest of the adult population? And isn't denying them that right, discrimination...since every other adult has that right?

Political Incorrectness

Many times, what is said or done in the name of political correctness
is just a means to avoid truth and fair play.

Political Tyrants

Did you ever notice that throughout history, almost all of the tyrants were politicians and almost all of the saints weren't? Mark

Twain once said, "There is a Congressman—I mean a son-of-a-bitch—but why do I repeat myself?"

Adam & Sid

Bob Cook, a good friend of mine from Decatur, Indiana, has one of the sharpest minds that I've ever encountered. He not only has many patents, but he has also been awarded a gold medal, from the prestigious Franklin Institute of Philadelphia, for his work.

Just to illustrate just how quick he is, one day I asked him, "Bob, do you know what the shortest poem in the world is?"

"Nooo."

"It's entitled *The Flea*," I said.

"The Flea?"

"Yeah, and it goes,"Adam Had'em."

Bob chuckled a little, and then I could almost hear the wheels start whirling in his brain. In just a trice, a twinkle appeared in his eye, and I knew something was coming.

"No it's not," he informed me.

"It's not? Well what is?"

"It's entitled *Died*."

"Died?"

"Yeah," he went on, "Sid Did!"

A Twenty's Not So Grand

In the early 1950s, Joe, one of the best dry-wallers in Adams County, was finishing a room addition in this rather attractive lady's home, when the subject of money came up. She went on to say how she would love to marry a millionaire. "Why," she said, "If I met a man with lots of money, I'd run off with him in a minute."

"I've got twenty bucks!" said Joe hopefully.

"That's not enough!" she indignantly informed him.

Moral: A twenty's not so grand to a gold digger!

How Far Will We Go?

Every so often, there is talk of taking driving and other privileges away from the elderly. All I can say is that we better be real careful how we treat our parents and the aged, for what goes around, often seems to come around.

When I was in high school (1948-1952), I lived in a foster home with a wonderful elderly lady by the name of Christina (Tienie) Schurger, and I can still remember this story that she told me those many years ago and I shall tell it to you.

Not too many generations ago, in the isolated rural areas of Russia, life was extremely harsh. It was truly a struggle, especially during the long, bitter winters, to have enough to eat and to stay alive until spring. Many times when the food supply was low, the father, to ensure that the children and contributing adults were able to survive, would load the grandfather, grandmother, and others too old to pull their own weight, onto a sleigh, drive them out to a secluded area in the sub-zero wilderness and leave them there to die.

On one occasion, when a son was taking his aging father on such a fatal sleigh ride, the old man shrieked, "Stop...stop!"

"Why?" asked the son.

"Because I only took my father this far!"

Parental Delusions

Many parents suffer from the delusion that their children can do no wrong, and are close to perfect. Another story that Tienie told me when I was but a young lad, illustrates this mindset best and it goes as follows.

A mother was watching a parade of soldiers marching by, hoping to see her son. When she finally spotted him, she cried out, "Oh, look. Everyone is out of step...except my Johnny!"

Sleeping Sounds

Ring...Ring.

"Hello, Jauregui's."

"Maxine?"

"Yes."

"This is Fry. Is Joe there?"

"He just went to bed."

"Can I talk to him?"

"He's sleeping."

"He is?"

"Yeah, I can hear him snoring."

Hahnie

In the seventh grade at St. John's, two of my children, Jimmie and Heidi, were in Mrs. Hahn's class. Every year on a specified day, parents were invited to come in to discuss their children's progress with their teachers.

Mrs. Hahn was my kid's homeroom and history teacher. After chatting with her about their progress, she insured my wife and I that they were doing great. As we got up to leave, I shook her hand and said, "Mrs. Hahn, I bet I know what your husband calls you."

She then gave me a curious look that I interpreted as either, how in the hell does he know, or who is this nut, but I continued anyway. "I'll bet he calls you "Hahnie!"

The Easy Way

My four years at John Carroll University taught me
that if you have a great teacher or professor,
you'll learn twice as much with half the effort.
Needless to say, I was all for that!

What is it?

I'm so old that I can remember when
a statue, or any other work of art, was put
in a park or public place, we could tell what it was!

Sugar Daddy

My daughter Rachel will be a freshman at Ball State University this fall. Tonight I met her at "Best Buy," to purchase a printer for her computer. After spending twice as much for a printer-copier than I expected, the salesman pointed out that we needed a thirty-dollar cable to connect the two.

Then Rachel said she needed extra ink cartridges, a black and a colored one: another fifty bucks. Next, she informed me that she needed paper. "Rachel," I said, "I'm your father, not your "Sugar Daddy!"

Boo-ick

My friend Henry Husmann came over to the United States from Germany, shortly after World War II. He couldn't speak a word of English, but learned it very quickly by reading the newspaper and watching television. One word that he had an extremely difficult time pronouncing was Buick. He would say, "Boo-ick," and his lovely wife Anne would try in vain to get him to pronounce it correctly, with little success. After years of trying, he finally got it right.

Several years ago, Henry, my son John, and I were planning a trip to Germany and I was trying to learn some German. I was having a rough time pronouncing the word Köln, (German for the city Cologne). Henry tried to help me, but after trying many times over several months I still couldn't get it right. Finally, in sheer exasperation, Henry looked at me and said "Köln…Köln…Köln…Köln!"

Annoyed at his impatience, I shouted back, "Boo-ick, Boo-ick!"

Major vs. Minor

Do you know the difference between major and minor surgery?

Major surgery is when they are operating on me.

Minor surgery is when they're operating on you!

No Matter How Humble.....

Did you ever wonder how many people are actually in jail or prison, because that's where they want to be? At least there, they know that they'll get three meals a day and a warm place to sleep. Not to mention other perks, like time to exercise, read, watch TV, and to get an education, if they are so inclined. Many such inmates would have difficulty providing these necessities and benefits for themselves in the outside world, so they are content in the confines of their cozy cocoons...compliments of Uncle Sam.

Cowboy

There is an old cowboy saying that goes,

"There's not a horse that can't be rode,

nor a man that can't be throwed!"

(Which tells me that even the best can be bettered!)

Gold Water

Years ago, when they started selling bottled water, I thought, that's nuts! Who's going to pay for something that you can get for free? Today, it is not only selling like hot cakes, but also a gallon of bottled water cost more than a gallon of gas, which brings me to the following conclusion. If we are willing to pay more for something that is free, than something that has to be found, pumped from the bowels of the earth, refined, transported, and then stored at convenient locations, so it's available when we need it at a cost cheaper than bottled water, perhaps we should never again complain about the price of a gallon of gas!

Dear John

This weekend, my son, Jimmie, and I went to Menard's Home Improvement Store, and looked at some outdoor carpeting for the screened-in-porch, that we recently added to our lake cottage. After picking out a couple of different patterns that we liked, I noticed that there were samples, about eight by eight inches long. So I asked the clerk, if we could have a sample of each carpet to see which one would be the most compatible with our porch's color scheme.

"They're 99 cents apiece," she informed me.

"I thought you gave samples away."

"John Menard said to charge 99 cents for them, and we have to keep John happy," she answered.

"Well, you know what I do to Johns, don't you?"

"What's that?"

145

"I sit on them!"

Pretty Memories

My wife Fry has a phenomenal memory, when it comes to remembering names. She can meet a person once and not only remember their name, but also their birthday. As for me, I have a hard time remembering names, but I'm good at remembering faces. Especially the pretty ones!

Not Up is Good

I don't care what my number is...as long as it's not up!

No Difference

On a recent trip to Mexico City, Mexico, we noticed that the population seemed to be a mixture of Indians, Blacks, Spaniards, Europeans and Asians. Having somewhat of a big nose, I asked our driver and guide, Roberto, if there was much prejudice in Mexico? He shook his head and said, "No."

Then, my son John pointed out the obvious, "Dad," he said, "In Mexico, it looks like almost everyone is a mixture of at least two or more races or ethnic groups, so they are pretty much all the same."

In the early 1950s, Father Henninger S.J., my sociology professor at John Carroll University, taught us that miscegenation (intermarriage between the races) is the only lasting solution to racial prejudice. He reasoned that if we all had a little bit of each race in us, there would be no one different enough left to hate...at least racially speaking!

Hippybottomus

Not all "Hippybottomuses," live in Africa!

Only 85

Two weeks ago, my eighteen-year-old daughter Rachel was picked up driving home from Ball State University, on I #69. When the arresting police officer told her that he clocked her going ninety-one mph, she indignantly told him that she wasn't going that fast.

"You weren't? Well, that's what I timed you at!"

"I wasn't doing ninety-one," she said emphatically, "I was only doing 85!"

Sinfully Good

The wages of sin…is a good time

…that one must pay for later!

Peanut Butter and Jelly

My children, Jimmie, six years old, Heidi, five, and Rachel, three, begged and begged me to get them a rabbit. After they promised me they would take care of it, I relented and bought them a medium brown male rabbit and a black female, for company. After a lot of discussion, the kids named the male, "Peanut Butter," and the female, "Jelly."

A few months later, Jimmie was playing with them in the foyer, between the garage and the kitchen. He had to run into the house fxor a couple of minutes, so he put Peanut Butter into one of the old style empty beer cases and closed the lid. When he finished his business in the house and returned to the foyer, Peanut Butter had escaped from the beer case and was doing to Jelly what rabbits are noted for. When Jimmie tried to pull Peanut Butter off Jelly, he hung on for dear life. Not knowing what else to do, Jimmie ran into the house crying, "Mommy, Mommy…Peanut Butter's stuck on Jelly!"

Horse Sense

A team of horses can pull a much heavier load than one,

but only if they are pulling in the same direction.

You d'Man

Throughout the history of mankind, women have always relied on men, since they are generally bigger, stronger, and faster, to provide not only children, but also food, shelter, and protection. As a result, this trait is so inborn, that no matter how hard the feminists try to instill in us the belief that a woman doesn't need a man, they will have little success. Because, by now, this instinct that was necessary for the continuation of the species, and was nurtured by thousands and thousands of years and countless generations, is so strong and imbedded so deeply in a woman's genes, that despite the feminists best efforts, they will not be able to eradicate it.

Definition of a Rat

Anyone that unexpectedly gives you a hamster!

The Bedpost Hang-up

Joe, somewhat of a chauvinistic blowhard and the father of seven, his wife, and a few other couples, were out one night on the town. After a few libations, during the course of the conversation when the size of Joe's fast-growing family came up, he proudly boasted, "Every time I hang my pants on the bedpost, my wife gets pregnant!"

Then Anne, who suffers fools lightly, sarcastically said, "Why don't you keep them on?"

Schindler's Closing Comment

I can only hope that you have had as much fun reading this manuscript, as I have had writing it. If the old saying is true that "the first shall be last, and the last shall be first," I suppose that this, my first book, is my last. Hence, my last book must be my first! Therefore, I can't wait to start the second! Thank you for your time, and Godspeed.

Printed in the United States
95263LV00004BA/1-99/A

9 781414 004846